OPEN HEARTS, OPEN MINDS

an anti-bias, multicultural curriculum for home and school environments

MEREDITH MAGEE DONNELLY, MS.ED

Book design by Meredith Magee Donnelly

Published by Homegrown Press

ISBN-13: 978-1984267542
ISBN-10: 198426754X

Printed in the United States of America.

DEDICATION

To Quinn, Luca and Charlotte- my dreams that came into this world with open hearts, open minds and strong spirits ready to take on this ride with me.

To Dave- thank you for cheering me on through this journey. You believe in me through every single "*hey, I have an idea*".

To my parents, Trish and Mike- thank you for teaching me to dream, look beyond myself and question the world. You have lived lives that demonstrate that with privilege comes the necessity to serve.

To all of you who have shared your stories with me. This is for you.

CONTENTS

When someone with the authority of a teacher, say, describes the world and you are not in it, there is a moment of psychic disequilibrium, as if you looked into a mirror and saw nothing.

Adrienne Rich, *Invisible in Academe*

INTRODUCTION

When I began my career as an educator 16 years ago I was under the false mindset that my job was to teach academic skills. And then I entered graduate school at Bank Street College of Education and started working with children. Children are organic beings and do not fit on a page in an academic curriculum guide. Like all people, children come to your learning environment with their own history, personality and learning style. I quickly learned that as an educator my job was to be the facilitator of learning situations, a protector of their emotional well-beings and a guide towards their own knowledge. My mission was to help slowly expand their worldviews, to see past their own experiences and have empathy and understanding of others.

I acknowledge that I am writing this curriculum as a white, heterosexual, privileged woman who does not have all the answers. I don't believe any of us should have all the answers. I am certain that there will be holes in this curriculum that will need to be filled by your own history, point of view and educational philosophy.

The following curriculum should be seen as a beginning. This is not where your journey as an anti-bias educator ends. You are a truth seeker. You are an advocate for all children. As such you will need to continue to educate yourself beyond this book and seek out more knowledge so that you can guide children as they navigate their own paths.

HOW TO USE THIS BOOK

The book lists and lessons provided throughout this curriculum are meant to ignite your thinking and creativity. Each section includes book recommendations and lessons. Use them as jumping off points to make the curriculum your own. You know your teaching style, learning environment and the children who fill it each day. Make each lesson the one you know your children need. Let their unique voices and visions of the world guide your path. Their questions will become your answers.

Though the lessons are broken up by age, this format does not need to be set in stone. Depending on how much experience your children have with this type of education you may want to adapt some of the lessons from the Pre-K to 1st Grade section for older children. With the exception of the first three lessons, the order of the lessons does not need to be followed chronologically or in isolation. Organize the lessons into your own unique schedule based on children's interests, mandated curriculum and time of year.

PRE-LESSONS
ANTI-BIAS SELF-AUDIT

Before you explore the anti-bias lessons with children take some time to focus on yourself. We all have our own biases. We come to educating young children with our own family experiences, personal history and education. The following self-audit is meant as a time of reflection followed by a time of action. You can simply answer the questions to yourself or write your answers down in this book, whatever guides your personal reflection best.

What are your earliest memories of noticing race? Were you part of the majority or minority? Do you continue to be part of the majority or minority?

Take a look at the books you read. Do they reflect the diversity of the world in terms of ethnicity, religion, gender, socio-economic status and sexual orientation? Would you feel comfortable taking the time to expand your book selections?

How often do you have the opportunity to have conversations with people of other ethnicities, races, religions, genders, sexual orientations or socio-economic statuses?

Do the television shows you watch reflect the diversity of the world we live in?

How often do you expose yourself to food from a different culture or origin?

How would you feel if your son or male student was wearing a dress? How would you feel if your daughter or female student shaved her head? Are your feelings based in fear? Are they based in taught gender norms?

Have you participated in religious events that are not from your chosen religion (or if you do not have a chosen religion)?

How often do you experience multi-generational activities?

Do you have the opportunity to travel to places different from where you currently live?

How do you feel about people currently immigrating to your country? Are you comfortable welcoming refugees to your town?

REFLECTION

What surprised you about yourself? What is one area of self-discovery that you would like to delve into deeper?

PRE- LESSONS

LEARNING SPACE AUDIT

After taking the time for self-reflection we will now switch our attention to our learning spaces. If you are school-based this will be your classroom as well as the general school environment. If you are home-based these will be the spaces you normally congregate to learn and play such as your living room, dining room or bedrooms. Unlike the self-audit, I am presenting this as more of a checklist with space for you to write quick notes on ways to improve your space. I hope this audit will show how simple changes can make a big difference in creating an anti-bias atmosphere. Please note that depending on the ages you are teaching and the type of learning environment some of these items may not apply.

DOLLS

Are they both sexes? Anatomically correct?

Do your dolls represent a variety of ethnicities?

If your dolls are wearing clothes, are they gender stereotypic?

BLOCK/DOLLHOUSE FIGURINES

Do the figurines pose the ability to have a variety of family dynamics? Two dad families? Two mom families? Dad/mom families? Single parent families?

Do the figurines reflect a variety of ethnicities? Can they represent multi-racial families?

If you are using figurines that have uniforms, are the ethnicities of the people balanced in blue and white-collar jobs?

Do you use wooden peg dolls instead of realistic figurines?

BOOKSHELF

Scan your current bookshelf. Does the literature reflect a variety of ethnic groups? Gender roles? Various parts of the world? LGBTQ families? Multi-racial families? Printed languages other than the language predominantly spoken in the classroom/home setting? Varying cognitive and physical abilities?

Do the books reflect different genres to appeal to a variety of learners? Graphic novels? Fiction? Non-fiction? Picture books? Chapter books? Cartoons? Magazines?

LANGUAGE

How do you address the children in your learning environment? Do you group them using gender specific names and pronouns (i.e. boys and girls)?

ART SUPPLIES

Do your art supplies allow room for a variety of ethnicities to be portrayed in the artwork? (crayons/paints in a variety of skin tones, paper choices, etc.)

HOME/CLASSROOM JOBS/CHORES

Are the children's jobs/chores gender stereotypical or are all children responsible for all jobs?

PHYSICAL EDUCATION

Are children exposed to a variety of physical education opportunities? Various team sports? Yoga? Dance? Are children separated by supposed gender identities? How are children paired for activities? Do you focus on integrating varying learning styles, abilities, and genders?

COGNITIVE AND PHYSICAL ABILITIES

Does your learning space honor the varying learning styles of children? Are there opportunities to stand and sit to learn?

Is there enough room and time allotted in your learning space to take breaks to move inside as well as outdoors?

Are there a variety of learning tools readily available to students to honor children who are kinesthetic learners, oral learners and visual learners?

REFLECTION

What surprised you during your learning space audit? What is one thing you could change today to improve your learning space in terms of an anti-bias education?

LESSONS

The following collection of lessons is designed specifically for the developmental ages of 3 to 7 years and 7 to 11 years. As you will notice, before we dive into lessons that focus on specific areas of diversity, we must first create a learning environment where all members of the community feel safe, listened to and celebrated. We begin with lessons centered on Listening, Caring for Our Community and Conflict Resolution. Once your learning community feels comfortable with these concepts, move on to the other lessons connected to your age group.

PRESCHOOL – FIRST GRADE LESSONS
AGES 3-7 YEARS

The beginning years of education are such a beautiful time for connection. As educators we must look at each child for his strengths and support his growth so that he will feel confident in his learning environment. When children feel good about themselves they will be able to feel good about treating their community members with respect.

We must remember that academic education is lost on children if we do not slow down and first focus on their emotional and social development.

AGES 3-7

LISTENING

When I was in college the best class I ever experienced involved a series of listening exercises. Being from a larger, rowdy family I had become accustomed to conversations that involved lots of talking over each other. The exercises began with simple 1 minute listening sessions working up to 10 minutes of sustained listening with nothing more than a nod allowed. It was during these sessions that I learned how to be both an educator and a student.

If the goal of education is to support children's growth into enlightened individuals we must first facilitate opportunities for them to learn to listen. We must open our ears to experiences and opinions different from our own so that we can grow together towards the common goal of accepting and loving this beautiful, diverse world.

READ ALOUD

Silence
Leminscates

GOOD MORNING GREETING

In a classroom setting, practice saying Good Morning around the circle. Model how to look the friend to the right in the eyes, smile and say good morning using the person's name. In a home setting, try it around the breakfast table. You can also add variety to this morning routine. Have one child per day choose an instrument to pass from person to person, or introduce saying good morning in different languages.

How does it make you feel to say good morning and have someone say it to you?

WHISPER DOWN THE LANE

Sit in a circle. Pick one person to make up a short sentence. The chosen person whispers the sentence to the person to the right. Now that person whispers to the next person until the sentence makes it all the way around the circle. The last person says the sentence out loud.

Was it close to the original? What could we try next time that would help us?

COMMUNITY INTERVIEWS

Choose 1-2 people each day to be interviewed. (If you are in a home setting you can do family members or friends). The community will ask five questions to the person being interviewed. You can brainstorm questions ahead of time. Practice eye contact and quiet listening while the person is speaking. After the interview each person will draw a picture of one thing they learned. Children can write a sentence or dictate one as well. Staple the pages together for quick and easy books about your community members.

LISTENING WALK

Take a quiet walk inside or outside your building. Focus on what you hear.

Try closing your eyes for a minute. Are you able to hear even more?

Without talking to your community members draw a picture and write a sentence (or dictate it) of what you heard.

Did everyone hear the same things?

LISTENING BOOK

Read *Polar Bear, Polar Bear, What Do You Hear?*, then create your own community Listening Book. This can be done in a blank big book or smaller version. Write each child's name on a page with the sentences, "Luca, Luca, what do you hear? I hear a ..."

Each child will have a turn to close her eyes and name one thing she hears in the room (or outdoor setting).

Keep the book available in the learning space to explore again and again.

PICTURE BOOKS ABOUT LISTENING

Howard B. Wigglebottom Learns to Listen Howard Binkow

Polar Bear, Polar Bear, What Do you Hear? Eric Carle

The Worst Day of My Life Ever! Julia Cook

My Mouth is a Volcano Julia Cook

The Rabbit Listened Cori Doerfeld

Lacey Walker, Non Stop Talker Christianne C. Jones

Silence Lemniscates

Listen, Buddy Helen Lester

Why Should I Listen? Claire Llewellyn

Listen, Listen! Ann and Paul Rand

AGES 3-7

CARING FOR OURSELVES & OTHERS

Early on in my career I was teaching my first graders Bob Marley's *Three Little Birds*. I noticed one of the boys in my class was becoming visibly angry. I asked him if he would like to share what was wrong. He said that the song was full of lies. He told me everything was not all right, and that he had real worries. He shared with me that his uncle was shot dead, that he was hungry most days. And there I sat as this privileged, white teacher in a predominately African-American and Latino classroom in a lower socio-economic area realizing I had completely messed up.

I came back the next day with a new song. I apologized to my students and told them I was listening to where

they were coming from. While I couldn't change everything in that moment, I could promise them that our classroom would be a safe haven. That day I taught them Bill Withers' *Lean on Me*. I watched them listen to me. I watched as they naturally put their arms around each other and started to sway. For the whole rest of the year we would start our day that way, with a song that became our battle cry.

This moment 15 years ago has stayed with me as I advocate for the importance of focusing on emotional health first, academics second.

READ ALOUD

A Sick Day for Amos McGee
Philip E. Stead

VENN DIAGRAM CARING CHART

A Venn diagram begins with 2 large circles that intersect in the middle. Label the circle on the left SELF and the circle on the right OTHERS. Where the circles intersect in the center is designated for SELF & OTHERS.

Have children brainstorm ways they care for themselves, ways they care for others and which actions help them care for themselves and others. Honor different opinions during this lesson.

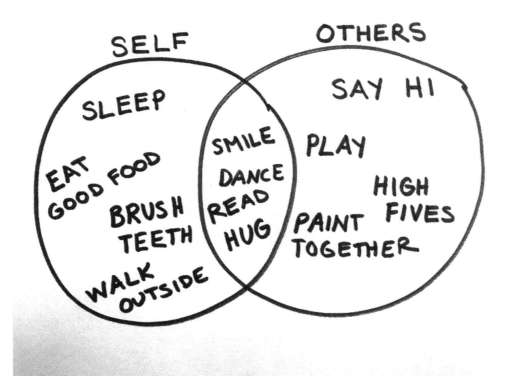

CARING CARDS

Brainstorm words and images that make people feel good.

Using simple white or colored paper folded in half, make cards filled with happy words and images.

Discuss who you could send them to such as people in a nursing home, children in a hospital, helpers in the community or family members and friends who could use a happy card.

I LIKE MYSELF DRAWINGS

Time to celebrate how awesome we all are! When we love ourselves and teach children to love themselves they feel good enough to treat others well too. When we treat others well, we feel great and want to continue the behavior. It is a happy, healthy cycle.

Read the book *I Like Myself* by Karen Beaumont. After reading the book have children brainstorm something they really like about themselves. Ask them to think about the best thing about themselves that instantly brings a smile to their faces. It is really important during this task that all ideas are accepted as equal. No answer is too small.

Give each child a large piece of white paper and access to drawing materials such as crayons or pastels. Make sure to include colors that are reflective of diverse skin tones.

Give children the opportunity to share what they like about themselves. Display the drawings on a prominent wall for all to see.

HUG JAR

Create a jar filled with soft felt hearts. Paper hearts are a good alternative. When a child feels that she needs some extra attention or love she can take a heart out of the jar and hand it to someone for help.

Alternatively, someone can take a heart and give it to someone in need of some extra love.

Keep the jar in a consistent place where it is accessible to children.

THANK YOU, HELPERS!

Helpers are all around us. In our daily routines we can get so use to these helpers that we forget to acknowledge how important they are and how much their actions are a demonstration of caring.

This lesson focuses on who is helpful to us in our daily lives. Give children a task at the beginning of the day to focus on who helps them throughout the day. Begin by discussing children's needs and how they are met. *How are you fed? Clothed? How was your home created? Who helps you learn? Who cleans your learning environment? Who makes you feel loved?*

Pause half way through the day, and then again at the end of the day, to reconvene as a group. Make a list of the specific people or types of people who are helpers in your lives.

Now it is time to tell your helpers how grateful you are to have them in your lives. Brainstorm ways you can demonstrate your appreciation. You can write thank you cards. You can surprise them with a meal. You can think about the hard work they do and what actions you can take to make their jobs easier. *What else can you do?*

PICTURE BOOKS ABOUT CARING

Please, Mr. Panda Steve Antony

Those Shoes Maribeth Boelts

Sam and the Lucky Money Karen Chinn

Last Stop on Market Street Matt de la Peña

Hey, Little Ant Philip M. Hoose

Have You Filled a Bucket Today? Carol McCloud

A Sick Day for Amos McGee Philip E. Stead

Rude Cakes Rowboat Watkins

A Chair for My Mother Vera B. Williams

Bear Feels Sick Karma Wilson

AGES 3-7

CONFLICT RESOLUTION

Learning how to confidently disagree with each other is one of the most important skills we can give our children. I never want children to feel like we all have to think the same way.

Honoring diversity means we will have moments of conflict. Perhaps our learning styles do not match up or our cultural backgrounds create a difference of opinion. Children need to know this is okay.

What is not okay is to make anyone feel less than for who they are or what they believe. When we stop listening to each other or start putting people down our hearts and minds shut down and we stop learning.

We must give children the tools to resolve conflicts peacefully and be advocates for each other during moments of conflict.

READ

One
Kathryn Otoshi

JUST BREATHE

Conflicts will arise within relationships, and it is important to teach children coping mechanisms to deal with them in a healthy manner. Being conscious of our breathing is one of the most important things we can teach children. Deep breaths trigger the brain to release neurohormones that give a relaxation response to the body.

Create a consistent practice in your learning environment of beginning and ending the day with deep breaths. Teach each child to sit comfortably, putting one hand on his belly and one hand on his heart, or placing hands in a prayer position or gently on the knees. Take slow deep breaths in through the nose and out through the mouth.

Talk to children about how they feel after taking ten deep breaths. Encourage children to use this strategy during moments of frustration.

Check in periodically on how the strategy is working.

ROLE PLAY CARDS

Print out the conflict resolution role play cards. Read a card and have children brainstorm what they would do in that situation. Write down the different options. This demonstrates to children that there can be many ways to approach a problem.

THE PAUSE ZONE

Sometimes we can't immediately solve a problem while emotions are flying high. Children need to learn that it is okay to walk away from a conflict in order to gain control. Create The Pause Zone in your classroom or home. This is a quiet corner that gives children the space they sometimes need. The spot can include items such as comfortable cushions, a basket full of fidget toys, music with headphones, a wobble cushion or small rocking chair and notepads and crayons.

This area should never be seen as a punishment, but rather used as a positive strategy towards healthy living.

Introduce the area as a place to go if you need a few minutes to regain composure. Ask for volunteers to practice going to The Pause Zone. Make positive observations about how the children use the area.

A BUG AND A WISH

One of the most important gifts we can give children is the power to use their voices. Children must feel empowered to speak their truth and state when something is bothering them. If we teach children to speak with strength and calm, we can curb future conflicts before they escalate.

In this exercise children are given the opportunity to state one thing that bugs them and a wish on how to be treated instead. Prior to introducing this activity read the book *A Bug and a Wish.* Following the reading give each child the A Bug and a Wish printable. Each child can write or dictate something that bugs him and what he wishes would happen instead. Have children draw a picture based on what they wrote.

Put the pages together to make a book. Read the book as a class.

Did anything surprise you? Are there any actions you can take to show you are listening to your friends/family?

CONFLICT RESOLUTION SORT

Read the book *What Would Danny Do?* This book is a unique spin on the choose your own adventure series. Throughout the book there will be moments to pause and decide the actions the main character, Danny, should take. With each decision Danny will be taken down a different path.

Print out the conflict resolution actions. Some of these actions have helpful solutions and some are not so helpful. Read one of the conflicts and have the children place it in the helpful category or not helpful category. Of course, there may be disagreements. Model how to discuss opposing feelings calmly using the lessons learned from the listening unit.

PICTURE BOOKS ABOUT CONFLICT RESOLUTION

Click, Clack Moo, Cows That Type Doreen Cronin

Stick and Stone Beth Ferry

Lilly's Purple Plastic Purse Kevin Henkes

Amazing Grace Mary Hoffman

Swimmy Leo Lionni

One Kathryn Otoshi

Stella Brings the Family Miriam B. Schiffer

The Butter Battle Book Dr. Seuss

The Lorax Dr. Seuss

Knuffle Bunny Too Mo Willems

AGES 3-7

LIKES & DISLIKES

As a child I remember being really nervous to share with peers what I really liked for fear of their reactions. I was at a friend's house one day, and we were given the option of tuna fish or hot dog. I really wanted a tuna fish sandwich, but my friend chose hot dog so I chose the same. There I sat eating something I didn't want because I was afraid to share my personal preference.

This memory has stuck with me for over 30 years. It would be easy for me to dismiss this memory as silly, but it has stuck with me because as a 5 year old that decision had an impact on me. It made me feel badly that I lacked the self-assuredness to make a choice that pleased myself.

I think about that time as I now educate children. I want children to equally ooze with self-confidence while celebrating the differences of others.

READ

It's Okay to Be Different
Todd Parr

LIKES/DISLIKES SCAVENGER HUNT

Have each child pick an item they would like to know if people like or dislike. This could be a food, a game, sport, book or TV show, to name a few.

Using the scavenger hunt template write the item at the top. Everyone walks around asking their friends or family members whether they like or dislike the item. Children can count the numbers in each column and share their findings.

The purpose of this activity is to demonstrate confidence in one's own beliefs and acceptance and respect of the beliefs of others.

BAR GRAPH LIKES

Creating bar graphs of your community's preferences can be an ongoing project and perfect as part of your morning circle routine. This is a great way to continue to support children's confidence in their preferences and acceptance of others.

Have a question available to answer such as *What is your favorite food to eat for lunch?* Make sure to include food items that reflect a diverse assortment.

Have each child answer the question by adding a unifix cube to her row or by coloring in a square in her row.

What is your favorite lunch food?

salad   sandwich   soup   other

LIKES/DISLIKES BOOK

Create a book that focuses on how we are different, but still care about each other. On each page focus on two people with opposing views. For example, "Charlotte likes vanilla ice cream. Desmond likes strawberry ice cream, but Charlotte and Desmond are still friends!

Use the book template provided to have children work in pairs to brainstorm something that they have different views about. Then have the children illustrate their pages.

Put the pages together to create the book "We Like Different Things".

MOVEMENT GAME

The purpose of this game is to learn about your community members, build confidence in oneself, and get those bodies moving. Tape a piece of paper with the word LIKE to a wall on one side of the room and the word DISLIKE to a wall on the opposite side of the room.

Have all the children meet in the center of the room. Before beginning the game, remind children that as a community we respect opposing points of view and treat each other with respect.

Name something that children may like or dislike such as pizza or playing soccer. When you name something, children go to the like or dislike side. If a child is unsure he can stay in the middle. Take a moment to have the children make 2-3 observations.

Repeat the game with a different like or dislike.

At the end of the game reconvene to discuss what the community learned about each other during the game.

PROUD TO BE ME
ART PROJECT

This project is all about encouraging children to be proud of themselves. When children feel good about themselves they will be more likely to treat others with respect and empathy.

Trace each child's body on a large piece of paper. Children get to fill in their traced bodies with all the things that make them proud to be who they are. They can use pictures and text. Use dictations for pre-writers.

PICTURE BOOKS ABOUT LIKES & DISLIKES

I Like Myself Karen Beaumont

Spaghetti in a Hot Dog Bun Maria Dismondy

10,000 Dresses Marcus Ewert

Sheila Ray, the Brave Kevin Henkes

This is How We Do It Matt Lamothe

Stand Tall, Molly Lou Melon Patty Lovell

It's Okay to Be Different Todd Parr

A Bad Case of the Stripes David Shannon

Same, Same, But Different Jenny Sue Kostecki-Shaw

Koko Rosemary Wells

AGES 3-7

OUR APPEARANCES

I grew up in the 80s- the time of color-blindness. As a child I remember finding this confusing. The message was that I could acknowledge the beautiful red rose, the turquoise ocean, but no, no, no, the beauty of skin color? Nope, not what we do.

Let's pause here.

What message are we teaching children to not acknowledge something like appearance that is right before their eyes? Are we teaching our children to be ashamed of their observations, or even worse, to be ashamed of how they appear?

In the lessons that follow we will celebrate the diversity of our skin tones, our hair, our eyes- in short, we will celebrate our appearances as a part of who we are. Our appearances will not be a ghost we look through, but a piece of the puzzle that makes us unique.

READ

All the Colors We Are
Katie Kissinger

MY PERFECT COLOR

Celebrate each child's unique skin color by mixing paints to exact matches. Give each child access to white, black, red, blue, yellow, magenta and turquoise paints. Model how to add small scoops of paint (spoons work great for this activity) to mix the colors. Explore as a group how white makes the colors lighter, and black makes the colors darker. After a group exploration, give each child a small jar, the My Perfect Color printable and a pencil. As children add different paint colors have them record what colors they are adding. This is a great lesson for practicing tally marks. Once the children create a match have them label their jars with their names. Keep the jars in a place they can be accessed during painting sessions. Children can celebrate their skin color paints by creating portraits of themselves on large pieces of white paper (see Self-Portraits lesson) or use the colors to create other pictures.

WHOSE EYES ARE THESE?

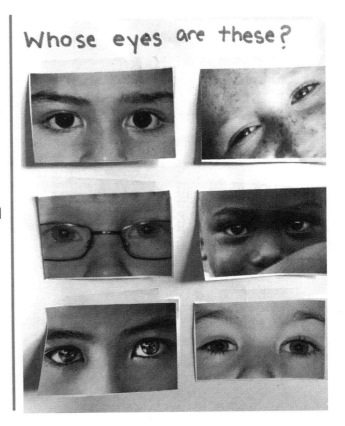

Print out pictures of each child's eyes. Fold cardstock in half and glue the pictures to the tops of the cards. Glue a picture of each child's face to the inside of the card with the child's name. Attach all the cards to a poster board or large piece of cardboard.

Can you guess who the eyes belong to? No peeking!

HOW TALL ARE YOU?

Roll out a large piece of butcher roll paper. Have each child lay at the edge of the paper. Tape a piece of yarn to the bottom and measure each child with a piece of yarn. Cut the yarn to the length of the child and tape it to the paper where the child's head is. Repeat with each child.

Discuss the findings as a group. *Are there any children who are the same height? Who is the tallest child in the group?*

How else can we measure each other? Try using unifix cubes or unit blocks to measure each person's yarn.

If your children are on the older side you could challenge them to figure out how tall they are as a whole group. *How will they figure it out?*

SELF- PORTRAITS

Self-portraits are a great way to send the message to all children that they matter. There are a number of materials that can be used for the portraits. Crayons, oil pastels, paints or paper for collages all work well. You could even have the different materials available and let the children choose which works best for them (provided that they have had ample opportunities to explore the materials). This is the perfect time to use the paints mixed in the My Perfect Color lesson.

As the children work make sure to provide access to mirrors so they can pause to look at their features. While working challenge the children to look at the details of their faces that are often overlooked. *What color are your eyebrows? Is this color the same or different than your hair? Look closely at your eyes. Do you see more than one color? Can you find a color (or mix a paint color) that matches your lips?*

Give children the opportunity to share their self-portraits. Make sure to create an atmosphere of confidence in each other's unique features.

ALL ABOUT ME SHAPE GLYPH

Glyphs are symbols used to represent information. In this activity children will use shapes to represent the different parts of their appearances.

Print out a copy of the All About Me Shape Glyph. Working together read through the sheet going step by step. *If you have wavy hair put blue triangles in one of the sections. If you have straight hair put purple triangles.*

Once completed, display the All About Me Glyphs. *Can you figure out who the glyphs belong to?*

PICTURE BOOKS ABOUT APPEARANCES

Whoever You Are Mem Fox

Red Michael Hall

Barry with the Fish Fingers Sue Hendra

Amazing Grace Mary Hoffman

All The Colors We Are Katie Kissinger

Spoon Amy Krouse Rosenthal

Elmer David McKee

Shades of People Shelley Rotner

Suki's Kimono Chieri Uegaki

Naked Mole Rat Gets Dressed Mo Willems

AGES 3-7

FAMILIES

The creation of a family study that truly honors and celebrates all types of families is what began my anti-bias education journey. I recently found an old email I sent to one of my students with two fathers. *"Hi, I am putting out books about different types of families, and I don't have any books on surrogates. Do you have any?"* (This was 14 years ago when it was much harder to find these types of books). The response to my email was quick. *Thank you. Thank you for seeing us.*

All children deserve to have their families truly seen. We are lucky to have such a beautiful assortment of diverse family books that continues to grow.

Use the book lists and the lessons provided as a platform to show your children that all families matter.

READ

The Family Book
Todd Parr

OUR FAMILIES BOOK

Begin by creating a book to celebrate everyone's families in your classroom or community. In addition to establishing a classroom/home library that reflects the diversity inside and outside of your community, making personal books about the children demonstrates to them that their lives are important. Invite parents or caregivers to bring in pictures of their families involved in a variety of activities, or volunteer to photograph the families if necessary. If you are not in a school setting invite members of your community or extended family to give you pictures of their families. Possible topics for discussion in the books are favorite activities, favorite family foods and members of my family. Children can dictate sentences that correspond with the pictures of their families. Read the homemade book to the children. Then make it available in your learning space.

FAMILY PORTRAITS

Continue the celebrations of all families by having each child create a picture of his family. Some possible art materials include pastels, watercolors, tempera paints or simple crayons. Make sure to include drawing materials that include diverse skin tones. Display the portraits in a prominent location.

Next have children choose to portray a family other than their own based on the books you are reading. Challenge the children to create as many different types of family configurations as they can.

FAMILY HOMES

Our diverse homes are also a part of us that should be celebrated. In this lesson children will build their homes out of blocks. If a child lives in more than one home, the child should have the option to build both homes. Give children access to accessories such as wooden peg people, fabric scraps, cardstock and markers to add details to their block building homes. If you don't have access to wooden unit blocks, Legos are a good alternative.

Depending on the size of your block building area choose a few children per day to create their homes. Take a home tour to give children the opportunity to tell the community about their homes. Photograph the block buildings to place in the block area. Label each child's building.

Enhance the experience by reading some of the following titles: *Home* by Carson Ellis, *Iggy Peck, Architect* by Andrea Beaty and *How a House is Built* by Gail Gibbons.

HOW MANY PEOPLE LIVE IN YOUR HOME?

Prior to introducing the activity label a piece of chart paper with the question *How Many People Live in Your Home?* At the bottom of the chart write the numbers 1-10, creating columns for each number. Draw vertical lines that go through each column creating boxes. Have each child color in a box that is associated with the number of people living in their homes. If a child lives in more than one home encourage the child to color in two different squares associated with each of their homes. Have manipulatives available to help children count. Discuss the findings. *How many people have 4 people living in their homes? Who are the people who live in their homes?* Observe how each child's family is unique. Even if people have the same number of people living in their homes, they may have a different makeup of people.

FAMILY RECIPES COOKBOOK

Food is a wonderful way to explore different family cultures. Send home a letter encouraging each family to send in one of their families' favorite recipes. If you are not in a classroom setting get recipes from your extended family or community members. Create a Family Recipe Cookbook. Throughout the course of the school year plan to make all the recipes in the cookbook. Encourage the child's family to join the community on the day the recipe is cooked. Give children the opportunity to sample the food. Alternatively, a family potluck dinner night would be a great school or community event.

PICTURE BOOKS ABOUT FAMILIES

BASIC FAMILY BOOKS

ABC A Family Alphabet Book Bobbie Combs

Who Is In My Family? All About Our Families Robie H. Harris

We Are Family Patricia Hegarty

The Great Big Book of Families Mary Hoffman

Families, Families, Families! Suzanne Lang

The Family Book Todd Parr

Families! Shelley Rotner

One Family George Shannon

Who's in a Family? Robert Skutch

LGBTQ FAMILY BOOKS

Molly's Family Nancy Garden

Heather Has Two Mommies Lesléa Newman

Donovan's Big Day Lesléa Newman

In Our Mother's House Patricia Polacco

And Tango Makes Three Justin Richardson and Peter Parnell

Stella Brings the Family Miriam B. Schiffer

Zak's Safari Christy Tyner

One Dad, Two Dads, Brown Dads, Blue Dads Johnny Valentine

Home at Last Vera B. Williams

DIVORCED FAMILIES BOOKS

Priscilla Twice Judith Caseley

My Parents Are Divorced, My Elbows Have Nicknames, and Other Facts About Me Bill Cochran

Fred Stays With Me! Nancy Coffelt

Two Old Potatoes and Me John Coy

I Have Two Homes Marian De Smet

I Don't Want to Talk About It Jeanie Franz Ransom

Mom and Dad Glue Kes Gray

Was It the Chocolate Pudding? Sandra Levins

Two Homes Claire Masurel

Oliver at the Window Elizabeth Shreeve

Living with Mom and Living with Dad Melanie Walsh

MULTIRACIAL FAMILES

Black is Brown is Tan Arnold Adoff

Marisol McDonald Doesn't Match/Marisol McDonald No Combina Monica Brown

Mixed Me! Taye Diggs

I Love Saturdays y Domingos Alma Flor Ada

Billy and Belle Sarah Garland

The Hello, Goodbye Window Norton Juster

You Were the First Patricia MacLachlan

Dumpling Soup Jama Kim Rattigan

One Family George Shannon

Jalapeño Bagels Natasha Wing

ADOPTIVE FAMILIES

Owen & Mzee Marion Dane Bauer

Tell Me Again About the Night I Was Born Jamie Lee Curtis

Star of the Week: A Love Story of Adoption and Brownies with Sprinkles Darlene Friedman

A Mother for Choco Keiko Kasza

Over the Moon: An Adoption Tale Karen Katz

I Love You Like Crazy Cakes Rose A. Lewis

The Red Thread: An Adoption Fairy Tale Grace Lin

We Belong Together Todd Parr

And Tango Makes Three Justin Richardson and Peter Parnell

The Red Blanket Eliza Thomas

SINGLE PARENT FAMILIES

The Storm Whale Benji Davies

Love is a Family Roma Downey

Kate and Nate are Running Late! Kate Egan

Raising You Alone Warren Hanson

Boundless Grace Mary Hoffman

Big Red Lollipop Rukhsana Khan

Two is Enough Janna Matthies

Molly and her Dad Jan Ormerod and Carol Thompson

Yoko Rosemary Wells

A Father Like That Charlotte Zolotow

MULTIGENERATIONAL FAMILIES

My Two Grandads Floella Benjamin

Grandma's Tiny House Janay Brown-Wood

Grandfather Counts Andrea Cheng

Last Stop on Market Street Matt De La Peña

Abuela Arthur Dorros

I Really Want to See You, Grandma Taro Gomi

The Hello, Goodbye Window Norton Juster

Bee-bim Bop! Linda Sue Park

What Can Your Grandma Do? Anne Sawan and Sernur Isik

A Chair for My Mother Vera B. Williams

AGES 3-7

GENDER IDENTITY

Gender identity is a highly misunderstood term. When a baby is born people inevitably ask, *"Is it a boy or a girl?"* This seemingly black and white question is actually filled with grey areas, and we should not force people into such defined terms.

Before beginning these lessons on gender identity I encourage you to take the time to further your own education on the differences between sex and gender and the fluidity of gender identity and expression. The main goal of these lessons is to encourage children to feel comfortable in their own perceived gender identity and gender expression. Here are some terms to keep in mind during this journey towards understanding.

sex: the biological term used to refer to anatomical and chromosomal characteristics to determine female, male or intersex

gender identity: how people perceive and label themselves

gender expression: how people outwardly show their gender. This may or may not fit with societal norms

cisgender: a person whose gender identity is aligned to the biological sex assigned at birth

trans: a person who identifies as a gender not aligned with the biological sex assigned at birth

gender fluid: a person who identifies as a mix of traditional genders and moves between the two

gender spectrum: description used to describe the concept that gender is a continuum and not solely male/female

READ

Who Are You?
Brooke Pessin-Whedbee

GENDER STEREOTYPES BAR GRAPH

As a morning meeting question or at circle time pose the question *Have you ever heard someone say something is just for boys or just for girls?* At the bottom of the chart paper write yes/no/maybe. Give each child the opportunity to place a unifix cube in the appropriate section. After everyone has a chance to answer discuss the observations. Begin with the more concrete observations like *How many people said no? How many people said yes?* Inquire if anyone who answered yes would like to share what they heard. *How did that make you feel?* Give children the freedom to lead the conversation.

EXPLORING GENDER STEREOTYPES

Collect a handful of kid clothing and toy magazines. Give children time to explore the pages of the magazines. Focus their attention on how the magazine is organized. *Are there sections for boys and girls? Why do you think the companies do that? Have you ever wanted something from a "boy section" if you identify as a girl or the "girl section" if you identify as a boy? Is there anything you would like to tell the company?*

DRAMATIC PLAY AREA

The dramatic play area is a wonderful environment for children to freely explore different concepts. As you continue your anti-bias work as an educator this is an important area to focus on as it often falls victim to gender stereotypes. One way to break down these gender stereotypes is to make the dramatic play area more open-ended. Instead of focusing solely on a kitchen area or a slew of princess dresses, switch things up by having hollow blocks or cardboard boxes, with accessories such as scarves, thin blankets and a variety of gender non-stereotypical picture books. By keeping this area more open-ended you are giving children the ability to use their imaginations freely. You can have baskets filled with accessories that you switch out frequently to focus the play on the current interests of the children. Examples include pretend tools, magnifying glasses, safety goggles, animals or pretend food.

GENDER STEREOTYPES BOOK

Once the discussions are occurring and children are beginning to feel their little voices grow strong, empower them further by creating a book entitled *What's a boy's thing? What's a girl's thing?* The book begins by questioning who gets to decide what people can look like and act like. The book declares that *We should choose to like and wear whatever we want! We should be whoever we want to be!* Print out the pages of the book provided. Each page contains text that the children illustrate. The tenth page is for each individual to create a page in the book. Make as many copies of page 10 as you need for each child. The text states *Some people say I can't _____, but that is not true because I know I can!* Discuss how each child will pick something that someone told them they can't wear or do because of their gender identity and then declare that can't be true because he does it. Children love this part of the writing exercise because it is an action step that makes them feel powerful.

Read the book to your class or home community and keep on the bookshelf.

I AM ME! WRITING ACTIVITY

This lesson will look beyond the labels of gender, instead focusing on who each child is as an individual. The purpose of this lesson is to demonstrate that labels cannot describe who we truly are. In order to learn about each other we must give each other a voice and a listening ear.

Prior to introducing the writing activity print out the I Am Me! sheet. This sheet includes sentence starters such as I am happiest when I _____. I am strong when I _____. Guide children by reading the sentences together and helping them write or dictate their answers. Each child can add a picture of himself on the sheet.

PICTURE BOOKS ABOUT GENDER IDENTITY

10,000 Dresses Marcus Ewert

The Princess Knight Cornelia Funke

Red Michael Hall

I Am Jazz Jessica Herthel and Jazz Jennings

Jacob's New Dress Sarah Hoffman

My Princess Boy Cheryl Kilodavis

Sparkle Boy Lesléa Newman

Who Are You? Brooke Pessin-Whedbee

Introducing Teddy Jess Walton

William's Doll Charlotte Zolotow

AGES 3-7

OUR STRENGTHS & CHALLENGES

I remember an assembly we had in elementary school that focused on learning about physical disabilities. The woman had puppets in wheelchairs and with arm and leg braces. The assembly was probably 45 minutes long. Those 45 minutes allowed the school to check the box of teaching about disabilities, and then we all went back to our day of teaching everyone exactly the same way.

What did I learn in those 45 minutes? Not much. It was a tourist way of looking at abilities- a me versus them scenario.

I am proposing that we approach physical and intellectual disabilities as a part of who people are, but not the sole defining characteristic.

The fact is that we all have strengths and challenges that make up our unique selves. When looking at the lessons in this section it will be important to look at the makeup of the people in your learning environment. The lessons will give the children the opportunity to look at their own challenges and what is helpful. The lessons in this section will give community members the opportunity to listen to each other in an effort to learn how we can all make each other's lives better.

READ

Can I Play Too?
Mo Willems

EXPLORING OUR SENSES

This lesson will help children explore what it is like to live without the sense of sight and how the other senses help people who are blind thrive.

Set up a station with a variety of food samples. Each child will have small servings on a plate. Blindfold each child and give them a plate of food. Ask the children what they could do to figure out what the food is. *Could they use their sense of smell? Touch? Taste?*

HELPING TOOLS

Often times children are afraid of the unknown or misunderstood. One way to ease these fears and make children more comfortable with people who appear different is to simply slow down and take the time to learn about these differences. This lesson focuses on shifting the mentality of seeing disabilities as a negative and instead focuses on the ways we all need help and how aids should be celebrated in helping us all function in a positive manner daily.

Prior to this lesson collect a variety of tools that help people throughout the day. Make sure to include tools that children usually see daily and tools children may not see everyday. You may include tools such as eyeglasses, canes, hearing aids, noise cancelling earphones, fidget toys, special cushions, weight vests and lap blankets. If you do not have access to the actual tools you may print out photographs.

Introduce the items and explain what each tool is used for and how it is helpful. Give children time to explore each material and the freedom to share if they use any of the tools or know people who do.

HOW CAN WE HELP YOU?

Connecting back to the lessons on caring for each other, create a list of ways we can show compassion to each other's challenges. *How can we support each other's hearts, minds and bodies?*

On chart paper create two columns- THIS IS HARD FOR ME and THIS IS HOW YOU CAN HELP ME. Give children the opportunity to suggest ways we can support each other and members of the greater community. If necessary, scaffold the conversation by giving an example.

For example, *Loud noises are hard for me. You can all help me by remembering to use quiet voices.*

SHINING STARS WRITING ACTIVITY

One of the goals of this lesson is for children to understand that a person's challenges or disabilities are just one aspect of that person's unique self. In this lesson children will look inward to focus on something that is difficult for them and how they are helping themselves. Children will fill in the writing activity sheet using inventive spelling or dictation. Children will then have an opportunity to draw pictures of themselves. This activity celebrates all children as shining stars!

ABILITIES COLLABORATIVE MURAL

Time to celebrate all that makes us unique and all that bonds us together. Begin by rolling out a large piece of paper (a butcher roll is perfect for this activity). Create a neighborhood scene that is representative of where you live. Include a simple road and buildings. Make sure there is ample white space. Attach the mural to a low wall where the children can easily access it.

Give children materials such as construction paper, markers, crayons, oil pastels and scissors to create community members that they learned about through literature and discussions. Explore how to create people. *Will you include their helping tools in your representation?* This is a great opportunity for children to notice that people with intellectual and physical disabilities need these tools sometimes and not others. Sometimes peoples' disabilities are not noticeable at all.

PICTURE BOOKS ABOUT PHYSICAL & COGNITIVE DISABILITIES

PHYSICAL DISABILITIES

My Three Best Friends, and me, Zulay Cari Best (blindness)

I See Without My Eyes Mark Brauner Hayward (blindness)

Off to the Park Stephen Cheetham (blindness)

Just Because Rebecca Elliot (use of wheelchair)

The Pirate of Kindergarten George Ella Lyon (double vision)

Moses Sees a Play Isaac Millman (deafness)

Kami and the Yaks Andrea Stenn Stryer (deafness)

Emmanuel's Gift Laurie Ann Thompson (leg deformity)

Susan Laughs Jeanne Willis (use of wheelchair)

The Seeing Stick Jane Yolen (blindness)

COGNITIVE DISABILITIES

The Alphabet War Diane Burton Robb (dyslexia)

A Friend Like Simon Kate Gaynot (autism)

Ian's Walk Laurie Lears *(autism)*

My Brother Charlie Holly Robinson-Peete (autism)

The Prince Who Was Just Himself Silke Schnee (Down Syndrome)

We'll Paint the Octopus Red Stephanie Stuve-Bodeen (Down Syndrome)

My Friend Isabelle Eliza Woloson (Down Syndrome)

AGES 3-7

AGEISM

I have seen first hand the importance of living a multi-generational life. My children have the pleasure of cooking with my mom, going on walks through the woods, having baseball catches with my dad and listening to stories from the past that I would not be able to tell them. All of our lives are richer for these experiences. These interactions also combat the negative visuals children often see in books and movies- the old, decrepit man, the scary, wart covered woman, the man hobbling with the cane. These are elderly stereotypes that media often perpetuates.

The goal of the following lessons is to give a voice to the aging population so that we may learn from them and develop long-lasting, positive interactions.

Like many learning moments, when we take the time to listen to real life experiences we can learn more than any book could ever tell us.

READ

The Patchwork Quilt
Valerie Flournoy

OLDER FRIENDS INTERVIEWS

Invite older community members into your learning environment for the children to meet and interview. This is a wonderful opportunity to welcome grandparents and members of the community that touch the children's lives so that they can get to know them better.

Prior to the interviews brainstorm questions the children can ask to better get to know the older friends.

Give each child an interview journal. After interviewing each person children will have a chance to draw a quick photo or couple of words to remember key points the person said.

OLDER FRIENDS WRITING ACTIVITY

Following each Older Friends Interview give children the opportunity to write a favorite fact about their new friends. Collect these writings to create mini books that will be kept in your library area so that the children can read them.

OLDER FRIENDS PAINTINGS

Following a collection of interviews, each child will paint a picture of the older friends. Give each child a piece of paper that is about 11 x 14. I love to start these portraits using either black pens or pastels and then adding more color with paints. This is a wonderful opportunity to move past the constraints of what older people look like and focus on each individual instead. As the children are working you can prompt them to add details by bringing up some of the facts learned during the interviews. *Does Walter love to cook? Where did Barbara say she likes to take her walks?*

Display the paintings for all to enjoy.

WHEN I'M OLDER WRITING ACTIVITY

Skip the stereotypical 100th day picture that often comes with simply drawing yourself as old as you can think of. I'm uncomfortable with the exercise of drawing yourself old or dressing up old as it often lends itself to surface level portrayals deeply rooted in elderly stereotypes. After reading picture books with positive portrayals of aging characters give children the opportunity to brainstorm what they will be capable of doing when they are older. Instead of focusing on appearances, focus on what skills and knowledge they will have acquired years from now. *Will they have traveled to a new place? Will they know a new language? Will they have invented something that can help others? Will they learn how to cook a new food?* Encourage children to shoot for the stars and dream big dreams.

Children can draw pictures of their beautiful aging selves.

BE A HELPER

Empower children by helping them brainstorm the ways they can be helpful to their older friends. Take time to think about the answers to the interview questions. *Are there challenges our older friends talked about? What can we do to be more supportive?*

Guide children by referencing answers to the original interview questions. *Does Barbara not have family living near her? I bet that can be lonely. What can we do to make her feel good? Would receiving mail be helpful? Could we invite her to be a classroom friend more often? Jay mentioned he can't hear as well now. What actions can we take when we are speaking to him?*

Write children's suggestions on a large piece of paper. You will be amazed at children's abilities to look beyond themselves when they are given the opportunity.

AGING CHARACTERS IN PICTURE BOOKS

Song and Dance Man Karen Ackerman

Our Grandparents: A Global Album Maya Ajmera

Verdi Janell Cannon

Abuela Arthur Dorres

Aunt Flossie's Hats Elizabeth Fitzgerland Howard

The Patchwork Quilt Valerie Flournoy

Wilfred Gordon McDonald Partridge Mem Fox

The Hello, Goodbye Window Norton Juster

Albert the Fix-It Man Janet Lord

Miss Tizzy Libba Moore Gray

Sitti's Secrets Naomi Shihab Nye

Mrs. Katz and Tush Patricia Polacco

Tortillas and Lullabies Lynn Reiser

Hot, Hot Roti for Dada-Ji F. Zia

AGES 3-7

HOLIDAYS

Holidays are an emotional topic in educational settings. This makes sense. Holiday celebrations are wrapped up in our own family's beliefs and cultural heritage. In an effort to not be exclusionary many schools have opted to omit holidays from their curriculums. I think we are doing a disservice to children when we ignore what is often an important aspect of their lives.

Instead of ignoring holidays all together the following lessons are an opportunity for children to share a piece of themselves that is meaningful.

It is important to note that some families do not celebrate holidays and may not be able to partake in this part of the curriculum. I encourage you to meet with these families prior to beginning these lessons to discuss how to move forward. Let these families be part of the decision making process.

At this age children are egocentric. They need to see their own family's holidays represented. Focus on food, music and décor. Young children are just starting to be able to see the world beyond their own and are not yet ready for the deeper meanings of individual holidays.

Please note, teaching a holiday should never be a child's first introduction to that particular culture. This creates what is referred to as a *tourist curriculum* where the only association with a group is an isolated event. If taught this way children often do not comprehend that a certain group of people live every day lives just like themselves. This is why at this age it is better to explore the holidays that are part of your learning community and venture into other holidays and worldviews with older students. Take the time to explore these lessons and adapt them to your own learning community.

READ

Celebrations of Light: A Year of Holidays Around the World
Nancy Luenn

HOW DO YOU CELEBRATE?

One of the goals of a multicultural, anti-bias curriculum is to help children see beyond themselves and form a deeper understanding of the lives of people in their community and in the larger world.

For ages 3 to 7 years the goal of this lesson is to have children feel proud of their own family culture and respectful of other people's cultures.

After reading some books about celebrations and holidays invite the children to share one of the ways they celebrate a favorite holiday. Record the answers on large chart paper with their names. *Do people celebrate the same holiday in different ways? Does anyone celebrate different holidays in similar ways?*

HOLIDAY FOODS

The food families eat during different holidays often is deep rooted in family traditions as well as religious importance. In this lesson children will share some of the food they eat during chosen holidays.

Children will have the opportunity to create the food using Model Magic, salt dough or clay. These food items can be displayed or used in a dramatic play area.

This is also a perfect opportunity to invite families in to your learning environment to cook holiday meals with children. Small groups can help with the cooking and then everyone will have the opportunity to sample the food.

FESTIVAL OF LIGHTS

A common thread between many holidays is the festival of lights. Diwali, Hanukkah, Winter Solstice, Christmas, Kwanzaa, St. Lucia's Day and St. Martin's Day all have a festival of lights. Gather the children in a circle and hand them each a battery-operated tea light or a small candle, depending on your comfort level and learning environment. Explain to the children that in many religions and cultures there is a holiday that focuses on the celebration of light or uses candles. Ask the children if any of them light candles in their homes as part of a holiday. Invite children to share their knowledge with the class.

Give children a circle of model magic or play dough to create a candleholder for their tea lights. Once hardened they can decorate with paint.

HOLIDAY VENN DIAGRAMS

One of the most fascinating aspects of holidays is the similarity many have with each other. The more we learn about holidays the less different they will seem and the more welcoming children and adults will be to diverse practices.

Throughout the year choose two holidays to explore in detail. On large paper create a Venn diagram with two holidays such as Diwali and Hanukkah. Prepare ahead of time by inviting community members who practice the holidays to share their knowledge. Picture books and appropriate websites can be used.

OUR FAMILIES' HOLIDAYS MURAL

Celebrate all the diversity of your learning environment by creating a Families' Holidays Mural. It is important to note that even if all the children in your classroom celebrate Christian holidays, for example, they will have their own personal holiday traditions that are not identical to their peers. This is important for children to begin to acknowledge that even within a seemingly homogenous group there is diversity of culture and thought.

Children can draw pictures of the favorite ways to celebrate with their families and friends.

Give each child the opportunity to then add her work to the large mural.

PICTURE BOOKS ABOUT HOLIDAYS

GENERAL HOLIDAY BOOKS

Lights of Winter: Winter Celebrations Around the World Heather Conrad

Kids Around the World Celebrate! Lynda Jones

Just Like Me: Celebrations Anabelle Kindersley

Celebrations of Light: A Year of Holidays Around the World Nancy Luenn

Celebrate! Connections Among Cultures Jan Reynolds

HANNUKAH

I Have a Little Dreidel Maxie Baum

The Miracle of Hannukah Seymour Chwast

Hannukah Lights Ben Lakner

Chanukah Lights Michael J. Rosen

Hannukah Haiku Harriet Ziefert

PASSOVER

The Story of Passover David A. Adler

Lotsa Matzah Tilda Balsley

Dayenu! A Favorite Passover Song Miriam Latimer

A Tale of Two Seders Mindy Avra Portnoy

More Than Enough: A Passover Story April Halprin Wayland

RAMADAN

Lailah's Lunchbox Reem Faruqi

Raihanna's First Time Fasting Qamaer Hassan

Amal's Eid Amy Maranville

Ramadan Moon Na'ima B. Robert and Shirin Adl

Under the Ramadan Moon Sylvia Whitman

CHRISTMAS

Christmas is Here Lauren Castillo

N is for Navidad Susan Middleton Elya and Merry Banks

The Night Before Christmas Rachel Isadora

One Starry Night Lauren Thompson

Christmas in the Barn Margaret Wise Brown

EASTER

The Easter Egg Jan Brett

The Country Bunny and the Little Gold Shoes DuBose Heyward

Easter David F. Marx

What is Easter? Michelle Medlock Adams

The Story of Easter Patrica A. Pingry

DIWALI

The Diwali Gift Shweta Chopra

Diwali: Holidays and Festivals Nancy Dickmann

Let's Celebrate Diwali! Anjali Joshi

Diwali Festival of Lights June Preszler

Diwali Trudi Strain Trueit

HOLI

Amma, Tell Me About Holi Bhakti Mathur

Ganesh's Sweet Tooth Sanjay Patel

Holi Lynn Peppas

We Throw Color on Each Other Kavita G. Sahai

Festival of Colors Surishta Sehgal

Holi Colors Rina Singh

KWANZAA

K is for Kwanzaa: A Kwanzaa Alphabet Book Juwanda G. Ford

Kwanzaa Lisa M. Herrington

My First Kwanzaa Karen Katz

The Gifts of Kwanzaa Synthia Saint James

Seven Days of Kwanzaa Angela Shelf Medearis

WINTER SOLSTICE

The First Day of Winter Denise Fleming

Iliana: A Winter Solstice Tale Walter Fordham

The Shortest Day: Celebrating Winter Solstice Wendy Pfeffer

One Short Day in December Lilith Rodgers

A Story of the Winter Solstice Harriet Ziefert

CELEBRATIONS
SHOULD THEY STAY OR SHOULD THEY GO?

If we are truly going to focus on an anti-bias curriculum we must address the inclusivity (or lack thereof) of celebrations. As an educator my goal in deciding to celebrate certain traditional holidays always centers on the question *What is best for all my students?* Celebrating Mother's Day in a classroom where students have two dads, are being raised by grandparents or have a single father doesn't make a lot of sense. The trend towards letting that child make a card for a "special friend" pushes that child into the category of being different than the rest.

I have included some alternative ideas to the traditional celebrations as I urge you to not add these celebrations to your curriculum simply because they have always been done, but because you believe they have an important place in an anti-bias curriculum.

HALLOWEEN

While I admit it is cute to watch children parade around in their costumes, Halloween celebrations put some families at an economic disadvantage in having to purchase costumes, can be overwhelming for children with sensory issues, is not allowed to be celebrated by certain religions and can reinforce stereotypes with certain costumes. An alternative to traditional Halloween costumes is to create costumes in school based on a book your learning community is reading.

THANKSGIVING

It is so important as educators that we stop perpetuating the lies of pilgrims and "Indians" in headdresses sitting together eating cranberry sauce, turkey and pie. Please reference the section on Thanksgiving on page 106. Skip the costumes, instead focusing this time of year on what we are thankful for and how we can give to others.

MOTHER'S DAY/FATHER'S DAY

Time for some soul searching. Please ask yourself why it is important to celebrate these days in a classroom setting. *Does it exclude anyone in your learning community?* If yes, it does not deserve a place in your curriculum. If you want children to focus on expressing thanks for those who care for them this can easily happen as you study families.

AGES 3-7

BEING AN ACTIVIST

Children are natural activists. They believe in right and wrong and focus on what is fair. I love facilitating opportunities for children to use their strengths for positive change.

The lessons and books provided in this section will help children see the many ways they can be activists. Some children may feel comfortable using the platform of public speaking. Others will want to focus on creating artwork that sends a message or writing a powerful, persuasive letter.

All of these chosen avenues are valued as we help guide children and build their confidence in believing that their opinions and actions are necessary for positive change.

It is inevitable that children will disagree. Honor these differences of opinion and teach children how to disagree with respect. Positive change can't happen if we close ourselves off from listening to opposing views. Positive change occurs when we find a balance between speaking our truth and being open to listening to the truth of others.

READ

The Day the Crayons Quit
Drew Daywalt

COMPASSIONATE DEBATES

Debating topics is an important skill to learn. Circle time questions are a great way to teach debating skills. Begin by posing a question each day that requires children to take a stand (though leave an option for people who are unsure as well). For example, the question might ask *Do you think we should eat lunch outside today?*

Give children the opportunity to write their names in the section for YES/NO/I'M NOT SURE. This first step in learning to take a confident stance is important as children learn to speak their minds.

Once each child has commented give children the opportunity to discuss their views. Remind children that only one person speaks at a time, and all views are honored. We can disagree with each other, but must be respectful at all times. Teach children to begin an opposing point of view by saying, *I hear you, but I disagree.*

WHAT IS AN ACTIVIST?

After reading a number of books from this section talk to the children about how each of these people are activists who were passionate about change. They all believed strongly in something and figured out ways to make a difference.

Pose the question *What is an activist?* Write the children's ideas on chart paper. It will be visible that there are many reasons to be an activist and many ways to do it.

WHO CAN WE HELP?

There are so many ways for children to be activists in their communities. Begin by simply thinking of who needs help and how you can bring about change. Start small. If you are in a school setting, think about how you can help your school. *Does your local community need help? Local park?*

Make a chart with three columns. At the top title them WHO, WHAT and HOW. Guide the children as they fill in the sections.

PERSUASIVE WRITING

As you continue to read both nonfiction and fiction books about activism the children will probably start to voice things that they find unfair or in need of change. Don't let that passion die. Meet it with action. A first step for our young activists is to write persuasive letters. Have the children pick an issue that is meaningful to them. Brainstorm WHO they can write to in an effort to encourage change. Within this letter the children will focus on WHAT the issue is and ideas for HOW to make positive change. This is a powerful exercise.

I AM AN ACTIVIST PICTURE

Celebrate the confident activists in your learning environment by creating Activist Pictures. Have each child think about a way she is an activist. Draw pictures depicting themselves as activists. *Are they writing letters? Marching in protest? Sticking up for a friend?* There are so many ways to be an activist.

PICTURE BOOKS ABOUT BEING AN ACTIVIST

Click Clack Moo: Cows that Type Doreen Cronin

The Story of Ruby Bridges Robert Coles

Drum Dream Girl Margarita Engel

We March Shane W. Evans

Malala Yousafzai: Warrior with Words Karen Leggett Abouraya

Hands Around the Library: Protecting Egypts Treasured Books Karen Leggett Abouraya

A is For Activist Innosanto Nagara

Mama Miti: Wangari Maathai and the Trees of Kenya Donna Jo Napoli

Separate is Never Equal Duncan Tonatuih

Harlem's Little Blackbird: The Story of Florence Mills Renee Watson

2nd - 5th GRADE
AGES 7-11 YEARS OLD

As children continue to advance through elementary school self-doubt and critique can begin to set in. It is crucial during these years that we educate with even more careful thought put into the emotional and social development of children. When children feel confidant in who they are as individuals, they begin to look outward towards treating others with respect and kindness. These years are to be nurtured as we begin to challenge our children to look beyond themselves towards the larger world and embrace the diversity that exists. These lessons will also ask children to look backward at history that is full of mistakes and hardships in order to learn from a history that at times treated people as less than human.

It is important to note that some of these lessons are geared towards historical events in the United States of America. Please feel free to adapt the lessons to historical events in other countries while keeping the same concept of learning from the past.

AGES 7-11

LISTENING

Before we can learn from each other we must learn the skill of listening. The following lessons give children the space and time to practice listening with community members and their surrounding environment.

Listening is not simply hearing the words someone says. It is honoring the person speaking by reflecting on their words and giving pause before reacting.

Children deserve to be heard and valued by their community. When everyone feels like their voices are equally heard we can move forward towards deeper learning.

READ ALOUD

Silence
Leminscates

LISTEN TO ME

This simple exercise is inspired by the work I did in a college class. While we worked up to ten minutes of active listening, here we will focus on one minute. It is harder than you think. Children will be paired with a partner. If you are in a school setting be conscious of pairing individuals together who do not always partner together. Tell children that they will be practicing listening to their partners speak for one minute. The rules are simple, the listener can nod her head, but she cannot utter any words of recognition. After one minute have the partners switch roles. To make this exercise easier you can give topic suggestions.

Come back together as a group. *Was it challenging to speak for one minute? Was it hard to listen without talking?*

COMMUNITY INTERVIEWS

Choose one person per day to be interviewed. This is a great opportunity to learn about the various people in your learning community. If you are in a home setting you can choose family members or friends. The community will ask five questions to the person being interviewed. Practice eye contact and quiet listening while the person is speaking. After the interview each person will choose one thing that they found interesting or surprising about the person. This will be depicted through writing and drawing.

LISTENING WALK

Take a quiet walk inside or outside your building. Focus on what you hear.

Try closing your eyes for a minute. *Are you able to hear even more?*

Without talking to their peers have children draw a picture and write a sentence about what they heard.

WHAT DOES MUSIC LOOK LIKE?

Give each child a large piece of paper and drawing materials such as crayons, oil pastels or paint. The goal of this lesson is to have children focus on different types of music and how it translates to the colors and images on a page.

Prior to the lesson choose 4-5 songs that represent different types of music. This is a great opportunity to introduce a diverse selection. Play each song for about one minute and encourage children to create whatever the music makes them feel.

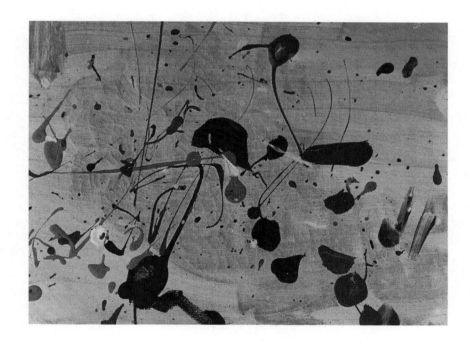

PAUSE AND LISTEN

Choose a time of day that is usually busy and on the louder side. This would be a time when people usually aren't focusing on the subtle sounds that are occurring around them. Get everyone's attention and tell the group to find a seat where they are and close their eyes. For 30 seconds have the children simply listen to the environment.

After 30 seconds have children share the sounds they heard. *Were there any sounds that were surprising or new? What made it easy to hear them?*

PICTURE BOOKS ABOUT LISTENING

The Market Bowl Jim Averbeck

A Handful of Quiet: Happiness in Four Pebbles Thich Nhat Hahn

Islandborn Junot Díaz

What Color is the Wind? Anne Herbauts

The Sound of Silence Katrina Goldsaito

Silence Leminscates

Listen to the Rain Bill Martin Jr.

The Word Collector Peter Reynolds

Charlotte and the Quiet Place Deborah Sosin

I Am Peace Susan Verde

AGES 7-11

CARING FOR EACH OTHER & OURSELVES

As I watch my own children navigate their social worlds, I can see they are pushing for independence and yet still needing my help with the big emotions and social interactions that don't always go the way they envisioned. These are the ages when we should be giving children space to form healthy relationships, while acknowledging that as educators and caregivers of children we need to carefully facilitate opportunities to explore these relationships in a safe learning environment.

Use these lessons as a starting point with the knowledge that specific activities about caring can occur throughout the year and non-formal modeling should occur daily.

READ

Those Shoes
Maribeth Boelts

VENN DIAGRAM CARING CHART

A venn diagram begins with 2 large circles that intersect in the middle. Label the circle on the left SELF, the circle on the right OTHERS, and then the part that intersects in the middle is designated for SELF & OTHERS.

Have children brainstorm ways they care for themselves, ways they care for others and the actions that help them care for themselves and others.

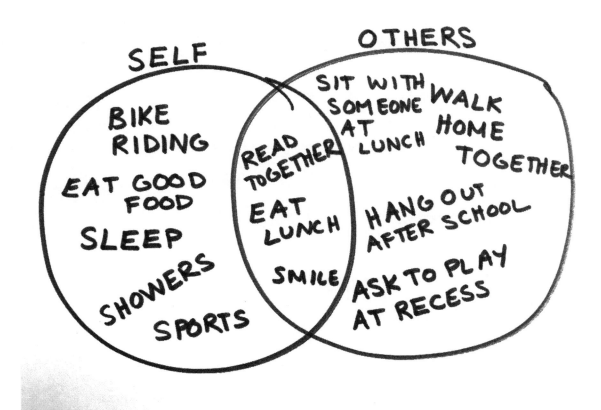

CARING CARDS

Brainstorm words and images that make people feel good.

Using simple white or colored paper folded in half, make cards filled with happy words and images.

Brainstorm who you could send the cards to such as people in a nursing home, children in a hospital, helpers in the community or family members or friends who could use happy cards.

I LIKE MYSELF DRAWINGS

Time to celebrate how awesome we all are! When we love ourselves and teach children to love themselves they feel good enough to treat others well too. And when we treat others well, we feel great and want to continue the behavior.

Read the book *I Am Enough* by Grace Byers. After reading the book encourage children to think about something they really like about themselves. Ask them to think about the best thing about themselves that instantly brings a smile to their faces. It is really important during this task that all ideas are accepted as equal. No answer is too small.

Give each child a large piece of white paper and access to drawing materials such as crayons or oil pastels. Make sure to include colors that are reflective of diverse skin tones.

Give each child the opportunity to share what he likes about himself. Display the drawings on a prominent wall for all to see.

SELF CARE

Balancing caring for others with caring for ourselves is an important skill to learn early. Give children the time to brainstorm ways they care for themselves. Make a list of ideas as a group. Highlight how each person's self care ideas will be unique to them.

Is there a self-care idea that someone else mentioned that you would like to try?

THANK YOU, HELPERS!

Helpers are all around us. In our daily routines we can get so use to these helpers that we forget to acknowledge how important they are and how much their actions are a demonstration of caring.

This lesson focuses on who is helpful to us in our day-to-day lives. Give children a task at the beginning of the day to focus on who helps them throughout the day. Begin by asking children what are their needs and how are they met? *How are you fed? Clothed? How was your home created? Who helps you learn? Who cleans your learning environment? Who makes you feel loved?*

Pause half way through the day and then again at the end of the day to reconvene as a group. Make a list of the specific people or type of people who are helpers in your lives.

Now it is time to tell our helpers how grateful we are to have them in our lives. Brainstorm ways we can demonstrate our appreciation. We can write thank you cards. We can surprise them with a meal. We can think about the hard work they do and what actions we can do to make their jobs easier.

What else can we do?

PICTURE BOOKS
ABOUT CARING

Those Shoes Maribeth Boelts

Sam and the Lucky Money Karen Chinn

Last Stop on Market Street Matt de la Peña

The Heart and the Bottle Oliver Jeffers

Ordinary Mary's Extraordinary Deed Emily Pearson

Pink and Say Patricia Polacco

Mr. Lincoln's Way Patricia Polacco

The Water Princess Susan Verde

A Chair for My Mother Vera B. Williams

Crow Boy Taro Yashima

AGES 7-11

CONFLICT RESOLUTION

One of the best things we can teach children is how to respond to conflict. Like any learning opportunity, this one will take careful thought, preparation, consistency and repetition. Children will learn how to voice their opinions with strength and empathy.

When we value diversity it is inevitable that we will have differing points of view. While diversity of thought is honored, we must make sure that our learning environment feels safe for all. This means having zero tolerance for bullying, excluding and name-calling. I am a firm believer in not allowing any of this behavior to go unchecked while acknowledging that this type of behavior has much more to do with how the instigator is

feeling about herself than others. This is why creating a learning environment that helps all children feel good about themselves is directly connected to how we react to conflict.

READ

One
Kathryn Otoshi

JUST BREATHE

Conflicts will arise within relationships and it is important to teach children coping mechanisms to deal with them in a healthy manner. Being conscious of our breathing is one of the most important things we can teach children. Deep breaths trigger the brain to release neurohormones that give a relaxation response to the body.

Create a consistent practice in your learning environment of beginning and ending the day with deep breaths. Teach each child to sit comfortably. Take slow deep breaths in through the nose and out through the mouth.

Talk to children about how they feel after taking ten deep breaths. Encourage children to use this strategy during moments of frustration.

Check in periodically on how the strategy is working.

ROLE PLAY CARDS

Print out the conflict resolution role play cards. Read a card and have children brainstorm what they would do in that situation. Write down the different options. This demonstrates to children that there can be many ways to approach a problem.

A BUG AND A WISH

One of the most important gifts we can give children is the power to use their voices. Children must feel empowered to speak their truth and state when something is bothering them. If we teach children to speak with strength and calm we can curb future conflicts before they escalate.

In this exercise children are given the opportunity to state one thing that bugs them and a wish on how to be treated instead. Prior to introducing this activity read the book *A Bug and a Wish.* Following the reading give each child the A Bug and a Wish printable. Each child can write something that bugs them and what the alternative action will be. Have children draw a picture based on what they wrote.

Put the pages together to make a book. Read the book as a class.

Did anything surprise you? Are there any actions you can take to show you are listening to your community members?

THE PAUSE ZONE

Sometimes we can't immediately solve a problem while emotions are flying high. Children need to learn that it is okay to walk away from a conflict in order to gain control. Create The Pause Zone in your learning environment. This is quiet corner that gives children the space they sometimes need. The spot can include items such as comfortable pillows, a basket full of fidget toys, music with headphones, a wobble cushion or small rocking chair and notepads, crayons and books.

This area should never be seen as a punishment, but rather used as a positive strategy towards healthy living.

Introduce the area as a place to go if you need a few minutes to regain composure. Ask for volunteers to practice going to The Pause Zone. Make positive observations about how the children use the area.

CONFLICT SUPERHEROES

Calling all superheroes! The world is full of conflicts and we need the help of kids! Have children brainstorm what characteristics a superhero has if her special power is helping people solve conflicts. Give children the time and space to create their own conflict superheroes. Children can draw the superheroes on pieces of white paper and then write some of the special characteristics.

CONFLICT RESOLUTION PICTURE BOOKS

Extra Yarn Mac Barnett

Draw the Line Kathryn Otoshi

One Kathryn Otoshi

Two Kathryn Otoshi

Bully Patricia Polacco

The Art of Mrs. Chew Patricia Polacco

Ish Peter Reynolds

After the Fall Dan Santat

The Dark Lemony Snickett

What Do You Do With a Problem? Kobi Yamada

AGES 7-11

WHO AM I?

I remember being 11 years old and deciding that I was going to wear as many different colors as possible to the Thanksgiving meal with relatives. I put on purple tights, brown corduroy shorts, a green shirt and a turquoise hat. Seriously. I felt like a million bucks. I recently found that picture and, admittedly, thought *whoa, that's a lot of look*. Here's the best part. No one that day made me feel silly about my choices, thereby giving me the space to let my confidence soar.

I hope the lessons in this section properly bottle up all the confidence I felt at age 11 on that day.

Children need us as their cheering section as they figure out who they are. Before beginning these lessons make sure you are far enough along in creating a safe, caring atmosphere that children will feel comfortable taking the leap to share about themselves.

READ

Sparkle Boy
Lesléa Newman

AMAZING ME GARLAND

As peers become more important, self-doubt and a critical eye on self can creep in. It is so important that we boost children up at this crucial stage of development. When we feel good about ourselves, we treat each other well.

Encourage children's confidence by having them write five things that make them unique and amazing. Give each child five strips of paper. Have the children write five things they love about themselves. Demonstrate all the different angles they can approach this pride- unique talents, kindness, ways they help others, unique characteristics, etc. After they write the five ideas on the strips demonstrate how to connect the strips to make a chain. You can then use additional paper strips to connect all of the chains together to display in your learning space.

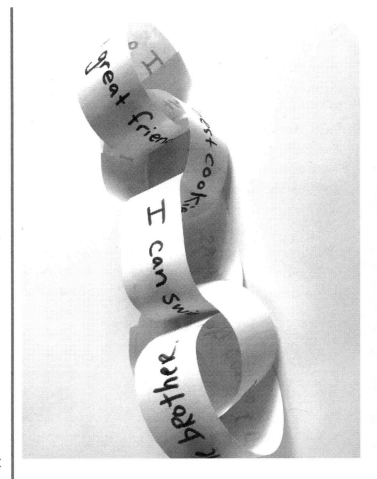

MY HEART

Guide children to look beyond their physical attributes towards the qualities they possess that make them wonderful human beings. Using the My Heart printout, have each child fill the heart with all her unique, wonderful characteristics.

At this age insecurities can start to stifle children's confidence. Our job as adults is to give them a supportive environment where they can feel good about the people they are.

MY PERFECT COLOR

Let's celebrate all the beautiful, unique colors that we are. Each child will receive a small jar. Baby food jars are perfect for this project. Prior to introducing the lesson have an assortment of paint colors ready for mixing. Colors should include red, yellow, blue, black, white, magenta and turquoise. Squeeze bottles are a great option or small containers with spoons. The book, *Shades of People*, is a great introduction to this lesson.

Demonstrate to the children that they will be mixing paints to make their unique skin colors while keeping track of how much they use of each color. If you are using squeeze bottles children will record the number of squeezes. If you are using containers with spoons children will record the number of scoops. You can use the attached printable and have children use tally marks to keep track.

Once children create their perfect colors they can label the jar with their names and display exactly how to make the color. Make the jars available to create beautiful paintings.

DEAR ME

Before we can fully help others we have to feel good about ourselves. In this lesson children will write letters to themselves where they offer compliments. Encourage children to look past appearances. *What are the qualities that make you a good person? How do you use these qualities to help others?*

This is a lesson that can be repeated throughout the year.

MIXED MEDIA SELF PORTRAITS

Self-portraits are a wonderful way to slow down and focus on the individual characteristics that make us unique and deserve celebration. Inviting children to use a variety of materials for the portraits further empowers them to make the best choices. Possible materials for the mixed media self portraits include paint, construction paper, buttons, felt, oil pastels, wood pieces and yarn. When choosing colors for the materials make sure to be conscious of choosing colors that represent diverse skin tones, eye color and hair color. This would be a wonderful opportunity to use the paints mixed in the My Perfect Color lesson.

PERSONAL IDENTITY PICTURE BOOKS

I Like Myself Karen Beaumont

Why Am I Me? Paige Britt

I Am Enough Grace Byers

Ada Twist, Scientist Andrea Beaty

The Name Jar Yangsook Choi

Spaghetti in a Hot Dog Bun Maria Dismondy

The Invisible Boy Trudy Ludwig

Sparkle Boy Lesléa Newman

The Dot Peter Reynolds

A Bad Case of the Stripes David Shannon

THE PAST

SOMETIMES ADULTS MAKE MISTAKES

In preparation for this section of the curriculum I did some soul searching about my own childhood education and reached out to others about their educations. It was blatantly obvious that there were gaping holes in how a majority of us were taught United States history. Many of us had at most a vague recollection of certain historical periods, while some of us had no recollection at all. The periods missing from our educations were the ones that did not paint the United States in a positive light.

As the United States continues to tackle racism, sexism, homophobia, transphobia, Islamaphobia, misogyny, and other forms of bigotry I am struck by the disservice we are doing to our society by not properly educating our youth about past historical events and how these events continue to affect our world. We cannot expect the world to become more open-minded and equal if we do not first embrace and learn from the mistakes of the past.

In choosing the historical topics I wanted to focus on ones that are often inaccurately taught, like Christopher Columbus and Thanksgiving, as well as areas that are not often taught in detail such as the Japanese Internment Camps and the LGBTQ Rights Movement.

These lessons should focus on historical facts followed by reflection, then action. *How could things have gone differently? What can we learn from these events?*

You will notice these lessons are arranged differently than the others. Each lesson begins with the historical facts. This is mainly for the adults to have a clear understanding before moving forward with the lessons. How you teach the facts will be up to you. I have included a list of recommended books that are a perfect way to begin. Following the books you can include class discussions and orally sharing more information. The lessons are meant to occur after reading the books and class discussions.

COLUMBUS SAILS THE OCEAN BLUE

If you grew up in the United States most likely the title of this section had you finishing the line with "in 1492". Like so many children I was taught about the great Christopher Columbus and how he discovered America. Unfortunately, this is not actually based in fact, and the real history is more complicated.

FACTS

Christopher Columbus was interested in exploring new lands. He originally attempted to get funding from the King of Portugal, but was denied in 1484. Years later in 1491 he received funding from the King and Queen of Spain with the agreement that he would receive 10% of the goods he brought back.

The trip in 1492 was much more complicated than anticipated. Columbus thought he landed in South Asia and therefore called the people living there *Indians*. He in fact landed in the Bahamas and was met by a group of people who were already living on the land called the Taíno. The Taíno people were skilled craftspeople. They gave the world peanuts, tobacco, cotton and hammocks. They are known for being artisans with ceramics, stone and wood. These people were unarmed, and Columbus believed they would make good servants. The Taíno people were forced into slavery. Some of the Taíno were kidnapped and taken to Spain to be slaves. Columbus and his men treated the Taíno people horribly and within a few decades the entire Taíno people were no longer alive.

In 1499 Columbus was arrested due to his horrible treatment of the people of Hispaniola colony of Spain that he governed. Despite the horrific actions Columbus took following his voyages, these voyages are considered crucial in the exchange of plants, animals, ideas, goods and diseases between the Eastern and Western Hemisphere.

DEAR CHRISTOPHER COLUMBUS

Empower children to learn from the past and take action. Have each child write a letter to Christopher Columbus. We cannot change his actions, but we can reflect upon them and take action to make sure we do not repeat them.

Give children the opportunity to share their letters.

TAÍNO PAINTING MURAL

The Taíno people are a rich culture of storytellers and craftspeople. After reading the beautiful picture books, create a list of what the children would like to include in the mural that would represent the Taíno people. Once the list is made decide who will make what. Roll out a large piece of mural paper (a roll of butcher paper is perfect for this). To help organize the space you could lightly draw out sections of air, land and sea.

TAÍNO PICTURE BOOKS

La Flor de Oro: Un Mito Taino de Puerto Rico/ The Golden Flower: A Taino Myth from Puerto Rico Nina Jaffe
Kiki Kokí Ed Roguíguez

CHRISTOPHER COLUMBUS BOOKS

Morning Girl Michael Dorris
Encounter Jane Yolen

THANKSGIVING

Where to begin with Thanksgiving? Out of any holiday research this is the one I find the most difficult to write about as there are so many lies associated with it that have become our real culture. Because of this these lessons will be sorted by facts and cultural lies and stereotypes. We will be looking at historical text side by side with books that that depict stereotypes and false information.

FACTS

Prior to the time period of what is taught as the Pilgrims, English explorers had landed in Massachusetts in the 1620s and returned to England with members of the Pawtuxet tribe as slaves. They left behind diseases that killed the people of the Pawtuxet tribe. Squanto, who was enslaved by the English, was the last remaining survivor of the Pawtuxet tribe.

The Puritans who left England and settled in Holland to escape religious persecution are whom we refer to as the Pilgrims. In Holland they did not find enough work or feel at home so they set sail for Virginia, but were forced to land in Massachusetts due to bad weather. Here they found the land inhabited by the Native American tribe called Wampanoag. The Wampanoag homes were made from branches and mud, not teepees as is often depicted. The Wampanoag did not wear headdresses or own horses. At the end of their first year the Puritans had a harvest celebration that is referred to as Thanksgiving. There is debate as to whether the Wampanoag tribe was invited to the celebration or they came as the result of the commotion from the celebratory gunfire. Unlike the Thanksgiving food that we now eat, this meal would most likely have included squash, wild turkey, venison, chestnuts and shellfish.

Word traveled back to the Puritans in England that the current Puritans in Massachusetts were living a peaceful life. As more Puritans arrived they began to try to claim the land, a concept foreign to the Wampanoag people who embraced community living. The newly arrived Puritans took over the land, enslaved the Wampanoag people and killed some as well. These Puritans continued to conquer more land and kill more Native American tribes. With each major battle and killing of a Native American tribe the Puritans would celebrate with a "thanksgiving". This is why many Native American tribe members refer to the current Thanksgiving as a day of mourning.

PROTEST POSTERS

After learning about the Puritan's treatment of the Native American tribes, like the Wampanoags, empower children to think about what actions they could have taken if they were alive when this was happening. Show photographs of some of the protests and marches that have occurred both past and present to challenge the mistreatment of human beings.

What type of poster could you create to protest the unfair treatment of the Native American tribes? What words and pictures would you put on your posters?

Give each child a piece of poster board and art materials such as markers, crayons or paint sticks. Children can work individually or in groups to create protest posters. Give each child the chance to share her work.

CREATING A COMMUNITY MEAL

The Wapanoag tribe strived to only use what they needed to use, avoiding waste, and living as a community on the land. This exercise will channel children to consider the feelings of Native Americans and their ancestors. Pose the question *How would you feel if you were living peacefully in a community and a group of strangers forced you off your land leaving you no place to live? Is there a way to shift the Thanksgiving celebration to be respectful of the feelings of current Native American tribe members?*

THANKSGIVING PICTURE BOOKS

Mayflower 1620: A New Look at Pilgrim Voyage Peter Arenstam
The Wampanoags Alice K. Fanagan
The Pilgrims First Thanksgiving Ann McGovern
...If You Sailed on the Mayflower in 1620 Ann McGovern
1621: A New Look At Thanksgiving Catherine O'Neill Grace
Tapenum's Day Kate Waters
Sarah Morton's Day Kate Waters

WOMEN'S SUFFRAGE

The Women's Suffrage Movement is one that often focuses on white women's right to vote in 1920 and the journey leading up to the success of the 19th Amendment. While an incredibly important part of United States' history it does not paint the full picture of the racial divide that was prevalent at the time. While white suffragists were fighting for the right to vote, they were not fighting for women of color. It is important we make the Black women suffragists at the forefront of this part of history.

FACTS

The fight for white women to vote began in the 1820s and would take 100 years to be put into law with the establishment of the 19th Amendment in 1920. It is important to note that this monumental fight for women's rights was solely for white women. While black men were technically given the right to vote in 1870, many systems were put into place to deny their rights. The equal voting rights of people of color would not occur until 1965 with the Civil Rights Act.

In 1848, a group of activists led by Elizabeth Cady Stanton and Lucretia Mott came together in Seneca Falls, NY. They believed that white women should have the same rights as men, including the right to vote.

It is important to note that women suffrage activists, like Elizabeth Cady Stanton and Susan B. Anthony, would not support the 15th Amendment that gave the right to vote to black men as they wanted the amendment to include all people. In fact they formed an alliance with racist white men who were fighting against black men's right to vote in order to push their own agenda.

Sojourner Truth is known as the first black woman suffragist. Truth, an emancipated slave, was known for speaking up for women's rights. She continued to advocate for the rights of black women and men until her death in 1883.

When the 15th Amendment passed, women of all colors felt defeated. Many women even denounced the suffrage movement declaring a woman's role was to care for her family and that voting differently than her husband would cause marriage problems.

In 1890 Elizabeth Cady Stanton became the first president of the National American Woman Suffrage Association. In 1910 some states began to give women the right to vote. On August 26, 1920 the 19th Amendment of the Constitution was ratified giving white women the right to vote.

Fannie Lou Hamer was a civil rights activist who was influential in getting people of color the right to vote in the 1960s furthering the work of Sojourner Truth 80 years prior.

INCLUSIVE VOTING ACTION PLAN

Challenge children to imagine they are fighting for their right to vote in the United States. *What would your action plan look like? Who would you be fighting for? If you could only gain the right to vote for people who look like you would you do it? Or would you continue to advocate for the rights of all?*

Using the actions of the suffragettes as examples, children will create five ways they will fight for the right to vote. Action plans may include speeches, marches, demonstrations and partnering with other people.

WOMEN'S SUFFRAGE MOVEMENT PICTURE BOOKS

Voice of Freedom: Fannie Lou Hamer, The Spirit of the Civil Rights Movement Carole Boston Weatherford

Ida B. Wells: Let the Truth Be Told Walter Dean Myers

Who Was Susan B. Anthony? Pam Pollack

Elizabeth Started All the Trouble Doreen Rappaport

Miss Paul and the President: The Creative Campaign for Women's Right to Vote Dean Robbins

Elizabeth Leads the Way: Elizabeth Cady Stanton and the Right to Vote Tanya Lee Stone

JAPANESE INTERNMENT CAMPS

I am ashamed to admit that I knew nothing of the Japanese Internment Camps until I was well into adulthood. How is it possible that I made it through all of my schooling and this piece of American history had escaped me? Unfortunately, I know I am not alone. It is difficult for adults to teach the painful aspects of history to children. This is a mistake. Children can handle a lot more information than we give them credit for. We need to educate them on the injustices so that children can learn from them and make better decisions as they grow.

FACTS

As a reaction to World War II and the bombing of Pearl Harbor by Japan, the President of the United States signed an executive order forcing all Japanese-Americans out of their homes and into internment camps where they would be forced to live from 1942-1945. Approximately 117,000 Japanese-Americans, who were mostly US citizens, were detained in these camps. It is important to note that prior to this event there was already a history of racism against Japanese-Americans.

Japanese-Americans, adults and children, had only six days to figure out what they were going to bring with them and could only bring what they could carry. These Americans were moved to camps that were not supposed to be lived in by human beings. Some of these were where livestock had previously been kept. Food shortages and poor living conditions were common. They remained here for months before being moved to permanent residences called relocation centers. These relocation centers were surrounded by barbed wire and had armed guards always on duty.

The legality of the Japanese Internment Camps was brought to the Supreme Court in the case called *Endo vs. the United States* in 1945. The Supreme Court ruled that the camps would not be allowed. All of the Japanese Internment Camps were closed by 1946.

PERSUASIVE POSTERS

One of the detrimental ways the government created hostility and fear against Japanese-Americans was to create racist, fear inducing posters and cartoons. After showing examples of these posters and cartoons empower children to create posters that combat the Japanese-American stereotypes. *What words and images convince people that the Japanese Internment Camps are wrong?* This activity will guide children in understanding the direct impact our words and imagery have on the opinions we form.

JAPANESE INTERNMENT CAMP PICTURE BOOKS

So Far From the Sea Eve Bunting
A Place Where Sunflowers Grow Amy Lee-Tai
Baseball Saved Us Ken Mochiozuki
The Bracelet Yoshiko Uchida
Fish for Jimmy Katie Yamasaki

CIVIL RIGHTS MOVEMENT

First things first, if the only time you teach about the Civil Rights Movement is in February for Black History Month it is time to expand your vision of education. As you plan out your curriculum make sure you are exploring key people in the Civil Rights Movement throughout the year. The historical events in the Civil Rights Movement are perfectly aligned with positive characteristics we hope our children embody.

FACTS

The Civil Rights Movement is generally defined as the historical events in the 1950s and 1960s, though it is important to teach children that to this date we are continuing to fight for equal rights. In order to understand this time period we must first have a firm understanding of the history of slavery in the United States and the subsequent laws that were put into place following Emancipation to keep people of color from being truly equal.

Following the end of the Civil War in 1865, 4 million former slaves were free. In 1867 Black Americans gained seats in the Southern State Legislature and US Congress. This period was known as Reconstruction. The 14th Amendment in 1868 gave Black people equal protection under the law, and the 15th Amendment gave Black men the right to vote. Many white people were not happy with the advancement of the rights of Black people. Jim Crow laws were put into place that made it illegal for people of color to use the same public facilities as white people. They were barred from living in the same areas or going to the same schools. In some states, laws were passed to limit black people's voting rights. In 1896 *Plessy vs. Ferguson* ruled that is was legal that areas for blacks and whites could be 'separate, but equal'.

Between the years 1882-1968 3,446 Black people would die via lynching. Lynching was a horrific, but popular action taken against freed Black people. The Klu Klux Klan was founded in 1866 as direct opposition to the rights of Black people causing terror and violence.

For the next 50 years Black people would hold the majority of low wage jobs such as farm workers, servants, maids, and factory workers. This changed during World War II. With pressure from the Black community wanting the right to serve in the military, President Franklin Roosevelt issued an executive order in 1941 opening up government and defense jobs to all people regardless of their race. Black men and women served in World War II, yet still returned home to discrimination. In 1948 Harry Truman signed an executive order to end discrimination in the military.

On December 1, 1955, Rosa Parks sat down in the Black section of a bus in Montgomery, Alabama. When a white man entered the bus and had no seat Rosa was ordered to get up, but she refused. Parks was arrested. This sparked Black community leaders to form the Montgomery Improvement Association led by Martin Luther King, Jr. This event began the Montgomery Bus Boycott that lasted 381 days. The Supreme Court declared segregated seating unconstitutional.

The Civil Rights Movement continued to push for equality this time focusing attention on the segregation in public schools. In 1954, the Supreme Court ruled that segregation was illegal in public schools with the case *Brown vs. Board of Education*. In 1957, 9 brave Black students made the attempt to start school at a formerly all white school in Little Rock, Arkansas. They were known as the Little Rock Nine. As they tried to enter school on the first day they were met with protesters. The Governor of Arkansas ordered the Arkansas National Guard to block their entrance to school. A few weeks later they attempted to enter the school again. They were successful, but met with violence inside. President Dwight D. Eisenhower ordered federal troops to escort the Little Rock Nine to all their classes. Even with this protection they faced continuous harassment.

On September 9, 1957, Eisenhower signed the Civil Rights Act of 1957 making it illegal to prohibit a person from voting.

Even with certain laws in place people of color received discrimination daily.

On February 1, 1960 a sit in began at a lunch counter in Greensboro, North Carolina to draw attention to the segregation of public spaces. This event was a catalyst for hundreds of people to also protest via sits ins as a form of peaceful protest. The Student Nonviolent Coordinating Committee formed following these events.

On August 28, 1963, more than 200,000 people took part in the March on Washington. It was at this March that Martin Luther King, Jr. would give his "I Have a Dream" Speech.

On July 2, 1964, President Lyndon B. Johnson signed the Civil Rights Act of 1964 that guaranteed equal employment for all, limited voter literacy tests, and made all public facilities integrated.

On March 7, 1965, a peaceful march led by John Lewis to protest the killing of a black man by a white police officer was met with extreme violence by the Alabama police force. This day is referred to as Bloody Sunday and was televised for all Americans to see. Despite this violence, Martin Luther King, Jr. continued to urge nonviolent protests.

On August 6, 1965 President Johnson signed the Voting Rights Act, banning all voter literacy tests, into law.

On February 21,1965 Malcom X was assassinated. Three years later on April 4, 1968 Martin Luther King, Jr. was assassinated.

The Fair Housing Act of 1968 prevented housing discrimination based on race, sex, ethnicity and religion.

Even with all this progress it is important for it to be acknowledged that discrimination and racism continues to occur on both individual and systemic levels.

CIVIL RIGHTS HEROS

The Civil Rights Movement is full of incredible, brave activists. This lesson will encourage children to choose a Civil Rights hero, research the chosen person and create a report. The picture books list below is a starting point, but should not be considered the only options.

Give children time to peruse the book selections and then make their choices. Once the child feels she has enough information on her chosen hero she will then pick a way to share the information. This could be in the form of an oral report, a painting, a collage or a PowerPoint presentation, to name a few.

Each child will then have the opportunity to share his findings with the class.

CIVIL RIGHTS MOVEMENT PICTURE BOOKS

Voice of Freedom: Fannie Lou Hammer Carole Boston Weatherford
The Story of Ruby Bridges Robert Coles
We March Shane W. Evans
Rosa Nikki Giovvani
Martin's Big Words: The Life of Dr. Martin Luther King, Jr. Doreen Rappaport
Sit In: How Four Friends Stood Up for Sitting Down Andrea Davis Pinkney
Boycott Blues: How Rosa Parks Inspired a Nation Andrea Davis Pinkney
The School is Not White: A True Story of the Civil Rights Movement Doreen Rappaport

LGBTQ RIGHTS

Discussion of the LGBTQ community and education is one that is often immediately met with opposition, but I ask that you enter this section with an open-mind. If you were turned off by the idea of teaching about LGBTQ rights I encourage you to pause and ask yourself what is causing your trepidation. Challenge yourself to consider that if we are truly to lead with *open hearts* and *open minds* then we must open our hearts and minds to all people equally.

FACTS

The first gay rights organization was created in 1924 by Henry Gerber. He created a newsletter entitled "Friendship and Freedom", but was met with police raids that forced the group to stop in 1925. The gay rights movement would go quiet for decades following this.

While we now know that people are born gay and there is nothing wrong with the LGBTQ community, in 1952 the American Psychiatric Association listed homosexuality as a form of mental disorder. In 1953, President Dwight D. Eisenhower signed an executive order banning gay people from federal jobs. This ban would stay in effect for 20 years.

In 1969, the police raided an establishment called the Stonewall Inn where the LGTBQ community was welcome to socialize. Frustrated by their mistreatment, individuals began fighting the police as their friends were being arrested. This is referred to as the Stonewall Riots. Protests would last five days. On the one-year anniversary of the riots, a protest march occurred on Christopher Street in New York City. This is considered the first Gay Pride Parade, an event that continues to occur every year.

These protests made way for some progress for LGBTQ rights. Several LGBTQ people became public officials. Kathy Kozachenko became the first openly gay woman to be elected into public office. Harvey Milk campaigned on a pro-gay rights campaign and became the San Francisco city supervisor in 1978. Milk had Gilbert Baker, an artist and gay rights activist, create a symbol for the gay rights movement. Baker created the rainbow flag that is the prominent symbol of the gay rights movement. In 1979, 100,000 people would partake in the March on Washington for gay and lesbian rights.

Like many groups fighting for equality the LGBTQ rights movement has been met with many ups and downs. Many LGBTQ people are bullied and physically hurt for simply identifying as part of the LGBTQ community. Others have been severely injured or killed because of their identity. In 1998, Matthew Shephard was tortured and killed simply for being gay. It would take until 2009 for President Barack Obama to extend the Hate Crime Act to include the rights of LGBTQ people. This is referred to as the Matthew Shepard Act.

In recent years laws were created that are helping LGBTQ people move closer to equality. In 2011, President Obama made it legal for LGBTQ members of the military to serve openly. In 2015, the Supreme Court ruled that states cannot ban same-sex couples from marrying. In this same year the Boy Scouts of America decided to no longer ban gay men from serving as scout leaders. And in 2017 they began to allow transgender men.

While much progress has been made, there is more work to be done towards equal rights in regards to work discrimination, transgender rights and businesses being allowed to discriminate against LGBTQ individuals under the veil of religious freedom.

RAINBOW FLAG

Create a huge rainbow flag that will serve as the backdrop for sharing facts about the LGBTQ Rights Movement.

Using a large piece of paper of cardboard, create six equal sections of the flag. Have the children paint them red, orange, yellow, green, blue and purple. Alternatively, you could have the children tape together pieces of construction paper to create the colors of the rainbow flag. If using paint, let dry.

Next have the children use black marker to write facts they have learned about the LGBTQ community. Children can also choose to write inspirational messages of acceptance. Display the flag as a symbol of acceptance and love.

LGBTQ RIGHTS MOVEMENT BOOKS

The Harvey Milk Story Kari Krakow
This Day in June Gayle E. Pitman
Sewing the Rainbow: The Story of Gilbert Baker and the Rainbow Flag Gayle E. Pitman
Pride: The Story of Harvey Milk and the Rainbow Flag Rob Sanders

IMMIGRANTS & REFUGEES

A connecting piece between all people living in the United States is that if traced back far enough all of our ancestors came from somewhere other than the US. Bones of people from 12,000 years ago are linked to Siberia 24,000 years ago.

We are a network of people with stories to share. The immigration of different ethnic groups has occurred throughout the entire history of the United States. Usually these people were coming to the US in search of a better life.

The question of our role in helping the lives of immigrants and refugees is as prevalent today as it has ever been.

There is no greater soul searching journey to take than to ponder how we should treat immigrants and refugees if we are truly living with open hearts and open minds.

READ

This is Me: A Story of Who I Am and Where I Came From
Jamie Lee Curtis

STUDY THE JOURNEYS

This will be an ongoing lesson as you read the recommended books. Before beginning your study of immigration put up a large paper map of the world that you are comfortable writing on. As you read through the different books chronicle the journeys the characters take beginning with their countries of origin.

Use a different colored marker for each character's journey so that children can compare and contrast the unique paths.

MY SUITCASE

Read *This is Me* by Jamie Lee Curtis. Imagine you are traveling to a new place and can only take what you can fit in a small suitcase. What would you bring?

Have a small suitcase on display so that children can reference the size as they come up with ideas as to what to bring. Using the My Suitcase printable, children will draw what they would include in their suitcases.

MY SUITCASE

ELLIS ISLAND POSTCARDS

After reading a selection of books about Ellis Island give children the opportunity to pretend they are one of the characters from the books. Children will pretend they have arrived in the United States and are mailing a letter to a family member or friend in their home country. *What would the postcard say?* Use the Postcard printable provided.

STATUE OF LIBERTY

This lesson will focus on the words associated with the Statue of Liberty which was a poem written by Emma Lazarus. Give each child a print out of the poem. Read the poem together as well as picture books such as *Emma's Poem: The Voice of the Statue of Liberty* by Linda Glaser

Explore less known words in the poem such as exiles, beacon-hand, yearning, wretched refuse, and tempest-tost.

Give the children time to read through the poem again and discuss what it means. *If this poem is to represent what the United States stands for, how should we treat people new to the United States?*

How can we use the words created by Emma Lazarus as a daily reminder of who we want to be as kind human beings?

Help children create their own poem representing the welcoming spirit of your learning environment.

REFUGEE AWARENESS

Empower children to make a difference by encouraging them to hold a fundraising event in your local community. This could be in the form of a bake sale, lemonade stand or local race.

This should occur once children have had ample time to read books and have discussions about refugees.

Some reputable organizations to donate to include the International Rescue Committee, Doctors Without Borders, Save the Children and UNICEF.

IMMIGRATION & REFUGEES PICTURE BOOKS

A Picnic in October Eve Bunting

How Many Days to America? A Thanksgiving Story Eve Bunting

The Name Jar Yangsook Choi

This is Me: A Story of Who We Are and Where We Come From Jamie Lee Curtis

The Matchbox Diary Paul Fleischman

Emma's Poem: The Voice of the Statue of Liberty Linda Glaser

The Colour of Home Mary Hoffman

My Two Blankets Irene Kobald

I'm New Here Anne Sibley O'Brien

At Ellis Island: A History in Many Voices Louise Peacock

The Blessing Cup Patricia Polacco

We Came to America Faith Ringgold

My Name is Yoon Helen Recorvtis

Stepping Stones: A Refugee Family's Journey Margriet Ruurs

The Journey Francesa Sanna

Angel Child, Dragon Child Michelle Maria Surat

Suki's Kimono Chieri Uegaki

My Name is Sangoel Karen Williams and Khadra Mohammed

Apple Pie 4th of July Janet S. Wong

All the Way to America Dan Yaccarino

BASIC
HUMAN
RIGHTS

The heart of the Universal Declaration of Human Rights is exactly what I am hoping we are teaching children. In 1948 representatives from all over the world came together to draft a set of protected rights for all humans.

The 30 rights are powerful to explore with children and pair perfectly with their desire for things to be fair.

The lessons in this section begin with learning about the human rights we all are meant to have and the activists who fight for our rights. We will then use these rights as inspiration to create our own learning environment rights.

READ

We Are All Born Free: The Universal Declaration of Human Rights in Pictures

Amnesty International

OUR HUMAN RIGHTS DRAWINGS

Depending on the number of children in your learning environment assign children the various human rights. Have children take the time to think about what the human right means and draw a depiction of it. The drawings can be put together to make a homemade book of human rights.

HUMAN RIGHTS ACTIVISTS

The Declaration of Basic Human Rights did not get created without hard work from human rights activists who continue to fight for the rights of people all over the world who are mistreated. Take the time to learn about the many activists who are working on different aspects of human rights. Have each child pick a human rights activist to research and create a report about. Children can display their research as a poster, a book, a speech, an art project or another creative way they come up with.

LEARNING ENVIRONMENT HUMAN RIGHTS

After learning about our human rights, challenge students to think about the rights we should have as people within a learning environment. *What rights should we have to make us feel safe when we learn? What rights help us learn in the best environment possible?*

Work together to make a list of Learning Environment Human Rights that everyone in the learning environment agrees on.

HOW WE PROTECT EACH OTHER

This lesson will reach the heart of the human rights created by the United Nations. At the core we are all human beings and need to take care of each other. After creating the Learning Environment Human Rights focus on the importance of treating each other with respect each and every day. We all deserve to feel safe especially when we take the risks to learn each day. The ultimate question is *How will we protect each other?* Pose this question to the children in your learning environment. Make a list of the actions you can take as a group to make everyone feel safe and accepted.

HUMAN RIGHTS MURAL

Draw a huge heart on a piece of paper. Using the individual drawings as a starting point welcome children to draw pictures or add words inside the heart that represent our human rights.

Keep this on display as a reminder of what to strive for.

HUMAN RIGHTS BOOKS

We Are All Born Free: The Universal Declaration of Human Rights in Pictures Amnesty International

My Little Book of Big Freedoms Amnesty International and Chris Riddell

Dreams of Freedom in Words and Pictures Amnesty International

For Every Child Caroline Castle

Peace Todd Parr

I Have the Right to be a Child Alain Serres

Every Human Has Rights: A Photographic Declaration for Kids National Geographic and Mary Robinson

Our Rights: How Kids Are Changing the World Janet Wilson

BEING AN ACTIVIST

There are so many incredible ways to be an activist. The following lessons will dive into what it means to be an activist while using literature to explore a range of historical activists. By studying a range of activists children will learn how the spoken word, protest marches, songs and education all play a part in creating change.

Children will embrace their own strengths and passions in creating their own action plans to promote positive change in an area of interest.

READ

Giant Steps to Change the World
Spike Lee

WHAT IS AN ACTIVIST?

After reading a number of books from this section talk to the children about how each of the people studied are activists that were passionate about change. They all believed strongly in something and figured out ways to make a difference.

Pose the question *What is an activist?* Write the children's ideas on chart paper. It will become visible that there are many reasons to be an activist and many ways to do it.

COMPARING ACTIVISTS

Pick two activists that have approached change in different ways. A Venn diagram provides a wonderful visual to easily see the comparison. Prior to the lesson draw two circles on a large piece of paper that overlap in the center. Write one activist's name on the left circle and one activist's name on the right circle.

Encourage children to discuss ways the activists were the same and ways they were different. The similar attributes will go in the middle of the circle. The differing attributes will be written in the circles where they do not overlap.

If there is interest this lesson can continue by picking two more activists. This is a great activity for invoking discussion and debate.

COMPASSIONATE DEBATES

Debating topics is an important skill to learn. Circle time questions are a great way to teach debating skills. Begin by posing a question each day that requires children to take a stand (though leave an option for people who are unsure as well). For example, the question might ask *Do you think we should take a walk in the rain?*

Give children the opportunity to write their names in the section for YES/NO/I'M NOT SURE. This first step in learning to take a confident stance is important as children learn to speak their minds.

Once each child has commented give children the opportunity to discuss their views. Remind children that only one person speaks at a time and all views are honored. We can disagree with each other, but must be respectful at all times. Teach children to begin an opposing point of view by saying, *I hear you, but I disagree.*

PERSUASIVE WRITING

As you continue to read both nonfiction and fiction books about activism the children will probably start to voice things they find unfair or in need of change. Don't let that passion die. Meet it with action. A first step for our young activists is to write persuasive letters. Have the children pick an issue that is meaningful to them. Brainstorm WHO they can write to in an effort to elicit change. Within these letters the children will focus on WHAT the issue is and ideas for HOW to make positive change. This is a powerful exercise.

MY ACTIVISM PLAN

These lessons in activism should be a catalyst for change within the children you teach, not isolated learning. Keep the momentum going by having children write an activism plan. *What are you passionate about? What challenges do you see in the world? How do you think you can use your talents to help change occur?*

This would be a wonderful journal writing exercise that could happen over the course of a year and, hopefully, beyond.

ACTIVISM BOOKS

The Story of Ruby Bridges Robert Coles

Drum Dream Girl Margarita Engel

We March Shane W. Evans

Giant Steps to Change the World Spike Lee

Malala Yousafzai: Warrior with Words Karen Leggett Abouraya

Hands Around the Library: Protecting Egypts Treasured Books Karen Leggett Abouraya

Mama Miti Wangari Maathai and the Trees of Kenya Donna Jo Napoli

Red Bird Sings: The Story of Zitkala-Sa, Native American Author, Musician and Activist Q.L.Pierce

Separate is Never Equal Duncan Tonatuih

Harlem's Little Blackbird: The Story of Florence Mills Renee Watson

LEARNING ENVIRONMENT AUDIT FOR KIDS

This is the ultimate lesson for empowering children. Give them the power to explore their environments with a critical eye looking towards positive improvement. Introduce this activity after the children have had ample time to explore the lessons throughout this curriculum. You can use the kid-friendly audit printable provided so that they can independently audit their learning environments. Come back together to share observations and ideas on how to improve the environment to be more inclusive.

BOOKSHELF

Scan your current bookshelf. Does the literature reflect a variety of ethnic groups? Gender roles? Various parts of the world? LGBTQ families? Multi-racial families? Printed languages other than the language predominantly spoken in the classroom/home setting? Varying cognitive and physical abilities?

ART SUPPLIES

Do your art supplies allow room for ethnic diversity? (crayons/paints in a variety of skin tones, paper choices, etc.)

SEATING

How often do you change seats? Are there a variety of types of seating or one type?

THE BEGINNING

There will be no *The End* in this book as the journey to educate yourself and those around you is never over. There are an abundance of questions to explore, the past to ponder and the future to create. We must enjoy the ride while always keeping open hearts and open minds. Thank you for joining me.

Now turn the page and begin.

ROLE PLAY CARDS

ages 3-7

Jaden is building a block tower. Maria takes a block from the top of the tower. Jaden is mad.

Matthew runs into line and gets right in front of Leah. She doesn't think this is fair.

Jeremiah is eating a ham sandwich. Alex says ham is gross. This hurts Jeremiah's feelings.

Tiffany and Xavier are playing on the playground. Jane asks to play and they say no.

Beth and Luca are dancing together. Luca accidently scratches Beth on the arm. Beth is mad.

Quinn and Charlotte are drawing at the table. They both reach for the red crayon at the same time.

Zayn is throwing a ball and accidently hits Mali in the head. She starts to cry.

Lily and Leela both want to sit next to Trevor at the table. There is only one seat available.

A BUG AND A WISH

It bugs me when you

_____.

I wish you would

_____.

CONFLICT CARDS

Danny yells and yells that he wants the ninja plate even though his brother Charlie is using it.

Charlie's snowcone falls on the ground. Danny chooses to share his ice cream sandwich with Charlie.

Mom gave Charlie new shoes because his old ones are too small. Danny wants new shoes. He yells at his mom.

At Danny's lemonade stand a girl knocks over his last cup of lemonade. Danny is disappointed, but chooses to help the girl up.

Charlie is playing a video game. Danny wants to play too. Danny chooses to watch Charlie play until it is his turn.

Charlie sneaks into the pantry and takes a chocolate bar. He eats it in the pantry.

Charlie is playing with his dog. Danny wants to play, but Charlie says no. Danny pushes Charlie into the mud.

While making lemonade, Danny gets lemon juice in his eye. Charlie starts laughing. Danny tells Charlie it isn't nice to laugh.

Do you like_____?

YES	NO

_____ likes _____,

_____ likes _____

but _____ and _____

are still friends!

ALL ABOUT ME
GLYPH

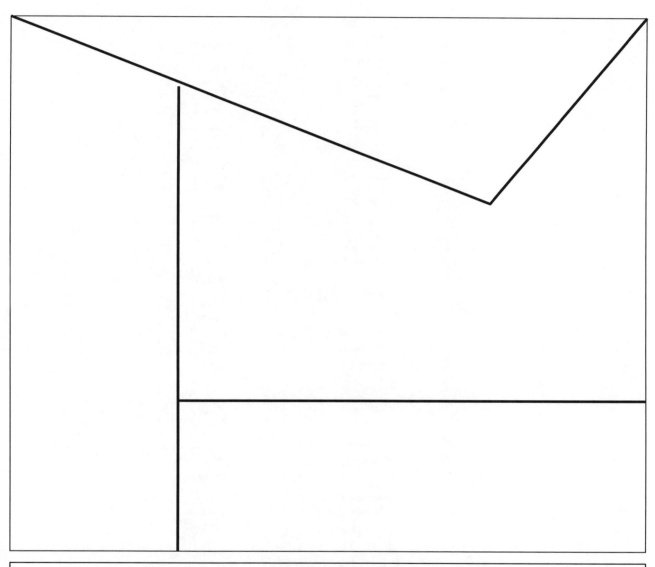

GLYPH KEY

straight hair – purple triangles
wavy hair –blue triangles
curly hair – yellow triangles

brown eyes –pink circles
blue eyes – red circles
green eyes – orange circles
hazel eyes – black circles

short hair- green lines
medium hair – brown lines
long hair – red lines

glasses – purple rectangles
no glasses – red rectangles

What is a boy's thing?

What is a girl's thing?

By: _____

What is a boy's thing?

What is a girl's thing?

Who gets to decide?

Some people say that only boys can like the color blue, watch sports or have short hair.

Some people say only girls can play with dolls, wear pink or have long hair.

We say, "That's not fair!"

We say, "People should choose to like and wear whatever they want!"

We do not let other people tell us who to be!

Some people say I can't _____

_____, but that is not true because I

know I can!

We say, "There is no such thing as a girl's thing or a boy's thing."

It doesn't matter what genders we are. We are all special people who get to decide what we like, no matter what other people say!

I AM ME!

I am happy when I _____.

I am strong when I _____.

I am proud of myself when I _____.

I find _____

challenging.

It helps me when _____

_____.

 I AM A SHINING STAR!

ROLE PLAY CARDS

ages 7-11

A friend in class calls you a mean name.

A group of kids are playing soccer at recess. They say you can't join in.

Jeremiah accidently spills his water on your math assignment.

Tiffany and Xavier start laughing while you are sharing the writing assignment.

Beth sees a group of children throwing Omar's hat back and forth. He keeps asking for it back.

Quinn and Charlotte are drawing at the table. They both reach for the red crayon at the same time.

Zayn is throwing a ball and accidently hits Mali in the head. She starts to cry.

Lily and Leela both want to sit next to Trevor at the table. There is only one seat available.

MY HEART

MY PERFECT COLOR

RED	YELLOW	BLUE
BLACK	WHITE	TURQUOISE
MAGENTA		

MY SUITCASE

Post Card

PLACE STAMP HERE

The New Colossus
Emma Lazarus

Not like the brazen giant of Greek fame,

With conquering limbs astride from land to land;

Here at our sea-washed, sunset gates shall stand

A mighty woman with a torch, whose flame

Is the imprisoned lightning, and her name

Mother of Exiles. From her beacon-hand

Glows world-wide welcome; her mild eyes command

The air-bridged harbor that twin cities frame.

"Keep, ancient lands, your storied pomp!" cries she

With silent lips. "Give me your tired, your poor,

Your huddled masses yearning to breathe free,

The wretched refuse of your teeming shore.

Send these, the homeless, tempest-tost to me,

I lift my lamp beside the golden door!

LEARNING ENVIRONMENT AUDIT

BOOKSHELF

Do your books have a variety of ethnic groups?

Gender roles?

Portray various parts of the world?

LGBTQ families?

Multi-racial families?

Printed languages other than the language predominately spoken in the learning environment?

Varying cognitive and physical abilities?

ART SUPPLIES

Do your art supplies celebrate ethnic diversity? Crayons? Paints? Paper choices?

SEATING

How often do you change seats?

Are there a variety of types of seats or one type?

Brainstorm one thing you can change about your learning environment to improve its diversity.

Meredith Magee Donnelly is an Early Childhood Educator with a Masters in Early Childhood Education from Bank Street College of Education. Meredith previously taught preschool, kindergarten and first grade in New York City. Meredith is a writer and owner of Homegrown Studio, an art play studio for kids. She resides in CT with her husband and three children.

Made in the USA
Columbia, SC
22 June 2020

12001457R00089